NEIL GAIMAN'S <u>THE SANDMAN</u> AND JOSEPH CAMPBELL: IN SEARCH OF THE MODERN MYTH

NEIL GAIMAN'S <u>THE SANDMAN</u> AND JOSEPH CAMPBELL: IN SEARCH OF THE MODERN MYTH

STEPHEN RAUCH

WILDSIDE PRESS

Published by:
Wildside Press
P.O. Box 301
Holicong, PA 18928-0301
www.wildsidepress.com

First printing: April 2003

Dedication:

For Joseph Campbell
I wish you could have seen this.

And Tori Amos and Neil Gaiman
For showing me the way.

Table of Contents

"Praise the world to the Angel, not what's unsayable. You can't impress him with lofty emotions; in the cosmos that shapes *his* feelings, you're a mere novice. Therefore show him some simple object, formed from generation to generation until it's truly our own, dwelling near our hands and in our eyes. Tell him of *things*. He'll stand more amazed; as you stood beside the ropemaker in Rome or by the potter along the Nile. Show him how happy a thing can be, how innocent and ours, how even sorrow's lament resolves upon form, serves as a thing or dies into a thing . . .

—Rainer Maria Rilke, "Duino Elegies"

"So I will lay on the highway, somewhere in New Mexico and wait for a strange light to come and take me home. Or I will stand by the statue, and wait for her to cry, I'd love to see a miracle once before I die."

—Jill Sobule

NOTE ON SOURCES

The entire run of *The Sandman*, seventy-five issues plus an extra issue (called a "Special"), is collected in ten volumes, plus an eleventh book that is not part of the original run. The volumes collect the issues as follows:

Vol. 1: Preludes and Nocturnes—issues 1-8

Vol. 2: The Doll's House—issues 9-16 (some versions also include issue 8)

Vol. 3: Dream Country—issues 17-20

Vol. 4: A Season of Mists—issues 21-28

Vol. 5: A Game of You—issues 32-37

Vol. 6: Fables and Reflections—issues 29-31, 38-40, 50, and The Sandman Special

Vol. 7: Brief Lives—issues 41-49

Vol. 8: World's End—issues 51-56

Vol. 9: The Kindly Ones—issues 57-69

Vol. 10: The Wake—issues 70-75

The Sandman: The Dream Hunters—published separately in 1999

In addition, there are two miniseries that focus on the character Death. Each is in three parts and each is collected in a single volume. They are:

Death: The High Cost of Living

Death: The Time of Your Life

Quotations from *The Sandman* are in the form of "Sandman [issue]:[page number]." Quotations from the *Death* miniseries are "[Name of miniseries], [part (1-3)]: [page number]."

As a final note, all the quotations that refer to *The Sandman* were meant to stand on their own. When the reader encounters them, it would benefit him or her to try to get a sense of the world of *The Sandman*, independent of my analysis. Of course, it would be even better to read the series before approaching the analysis—I would highly recommend this course—although this is intended to make sense to people unfamiliar with the series, as well as devoted fans.

INTRODUCTION: LIVING IN
A DESCRALIZED WORLD

"I love religion and I love myth. People say 'Why?' and the only answer I can give is because I'm me."

—Neil Gaiman

"If you need me, me and Neil'll be hangin' out with the Dream-King."

—Tori Amos

We are living in an age of wonders. Although the "Age of Reason" came hundreds of years ago, the fruits of reason have continued to grow, and we stand at the edge of a new millennium in a time of unimagined scientific progress. However, many would argue that this progress has come at a price. No one would question the usefulness of what we have learned, but just as we collectively turned toward reason, we have turned away from religion. Many of the old religious creeds now seem outdated, the products of another age, and it may seem that nothing has emerged to take their place. People live in cities of massive scale, yet are essentially cut off from true human contact with those who are closest to them. And people are learning that although we can do more than we had ever imagined, life without faith, without meaning, loses its essential vitality. Years ago, Nietzsche called this phenomenon the death of God, and we are still trying to come to terms with the meaning of that statement. And now it seems that, after having killed God, we are beginning to wonder whether it was a good idea.

Mircea Eliade, in his seminal work *The Sacred and the Profane*, sets out the spiritual problem of modern humans. His essential dichotomy of religious life is of the profane, the time and space of everyday life, and the *sacred*, that which exists behind ordinary life and supports it. It is the sacred that is essential for religious people. But modern people have to a large extent desacralized their world. Eliade writes about the modern situation, "the sacred is the prime obstacle to his freedom. He will become himself only when he is totally demysticized. He will not be truly free until he has killed the last god" (203). He describes such people as "without religious feeling . . . the [person] who lives, or wishes to live, in a desacralized world" (13). For Eliade, this is not an equal alternative to spiritual life, but is a significantly reduced way to live. He writes that profane acts "are deprived of spiritual significance, hence deprived of their truly human dimension" (168).

Others have followed Eliade in delimiting the spiritual problem of modern life. Lawrence Jaffe, a critic of modernity, says that "We are living in an era of unparalleled impoverishment and depreciation of the human soul. The collapse of our religious forms has been followed by a general demoralization of the dominant (Western) culture. No myth remains to sustain us" (7). He continues, that "people are beginning to bump up against the limits of materialism and rationalism, realizing that these fail to offer something essential, a purpose in life . . . We cannot do without meaning in our lives. Meaning cannot be established objectively; it arises only through a relationship with the inner, subjective world" (Jaffe 7). We shall see that inner worlds are very important, and the meaning they bring is something we cannot live without. Reinhold Niebuhr posits the issue of finding meaning as "the basic problem of religion" (I, 164). Also, Robert Johnson, in *The Fisher King and the Handless Maiden*, talks about the "feeling function"; "to lose one's feeling function is thus to lose one of the most precious human faculties, perhaps the one that makes us most human . . . The feeling function is a casualty of our modern way of life" (4). In his study, Johnson examines the story of the Fisher King in the Waste Land story as indicative of the modern condition. For our purposes, we will note that he speaks of many of the same things, as "the ache of life, the anxiety, dread, loneliness, the corners of the mouth pointing down— all are summed up by the fisher king wound" (22). Many of the aspects Johnson highlights: anxiety, loneliness, and meaninglessness, are characteristic of the modern human condition. And his theme of wounding has been picked up in the popular imagination, as people talk about the "walking wounded."

Paul Tillich also comments on modern life, as "the anxiety of doubt and meaninglessness is, as we have seen, the anxiety of our period" (142). Tillich also discusses the thought and art of existentialism, in which we see "all-pervading anxiety of doubt and meaninglessness. It is the expression of our own situation" (126). He adds that in our age, "the anxiety of emptiness and meaninglessness is dominant. We are under the threat of spiritual nonbeing" (Tillich 62). He also talks about the situation that occurs when religious and moral traditions are no longer relevant in people's lives, that "in such circumstances a slow process of waste of the spiritual contents occurs, unnoticeable in the beginning, realized with a shock as it progresses, producing the anxiety of meaninglessness at its end" (Tillich 50). Finally, James Hollis summarizes the situation, that "the old authorities have lost their power and the maps are missing" (109). The implication of this is that we are, in effect, lost.

Finally, religious scholar Huston Smith has added his opinion, in *Why Religion Matters*. He says that "the East and West are going through a single common crisis whose cause is the spiritual condition of the modern world. That condition is characterized by loss—the loss of religious certainties and of transcendence with its larger horizons . . . [when science became dominant], meaning began to ebb and the stature of humanity to diminish" (1). He also states that "the finitude of mundane existence cannot satisfy the human heart completely. Built into the human makeup is a longing for a 'more' that the world of everyday experience cannot requite" (3). Thus, there exists a human *need* for meaning in life. Similarly, he adds that "the traditional worldview is preferable to the one that now encloses us because it allows for the fulfillment of the basic longing that lies in the depths of the human heart . . . Whether we realize it or not, simply to be human is to long for release from mundane existence, with its confining walls of finitude and mortality" (28). Finally, he pronounces that "as for the scientific worldview, there is no way that a happy ending can be worked into it" (36). Smith's formulation might be a more negative view than we have to take, but he clearly feels the ache of modernity.

However, despite some gloomy assessments of our situation, there is hope. Eliade observes that for even the most profane of moderns, life is not without some survival of the sacred, as "the man who has made his choice in favor of a profane life never succeeds in completely doing away with religious behavior . . . even the most desacralized existence still preserves traces of a religious valorization of the world" (23). The sacred is alive in *us*, and while Eliade sees these phenomena as a faint reflection of the transcendent glory that belonged to *homo religiousis*, I would argue that the tendency towards the sacred, which one might even call an *instinct*, is still a vital force, and it forms the basis of the present study. And there is always hope.

So if we accept the formulations that our lives have become dry and meaningless, the next question to ask is how we should go about reclaiming that meaning. One of the primary ways that people in ancient (and even not-so-ancient) societies reaffirmed their roots in religious experience was through myth. When the first people sat around the fire, trying to keep the darkness at bay, there was myth. From the available evidence, it appears that myth has supported human endeavors for thousands of years. Paul Ricoeur speaks of myth as "an antidote to distress" (Symbolism of Evil 167). Still, this brings up the question: what is myth? The simplest answer is "stories about gods," and although this definition excludes quasi-immortals and demigods, perhaps it is a good place to start. But even mentioning myth here requires a leap of faith. Most of us know myths primarily from the old Greek stories; After all, stories of Zeus running around and bedding mortal women may have worked in Ancient Greece, but what relevance do they have today?

But this view of myth is little more than a caricature, and a number of modern scholars have taken myth to be narratives filled with ancient wisdom, stories that, if one knows how to look, teach us the meaning of life. The most well-known of these scholars of the last half century was Joseph Campbell. He once said that "it would not be too much to say that the myth is the secret opening through which the inexhaustible energies of the cosmos pour into human cultural manifestation" (Hero with a Thousand Faces 3). And although this view is filled with wonder, it is also rather abstract. Later, he would clarify his point, that "I think that what we're seeking is an experience of being alive, so that our life experiences on the purely physical plane will have resonances within our innermost being and reality, so that we actually feel the rapture of being alive" (Power 5). His point about the *experience* of being alive brings us closer to something we can use, but it still remains to be seen how stories about gods can evoke this kind of response in a reader. Campbell, more than any other scholar, will guide us throughout our journey.

Perhaps the best way to do this is by looking at what myth does. Campbell lays out what he calls the "four functions of mythology." The first is the mystical, to put one in touch with the wonder of the universe, as "realizing what a wonder the universe is, and what a wonder you are, and experiencing awe before this mystery. Myth opens the world to the dimension of mystery, to the realization of the mystery that underlies all forms" (Power 31). The second function is the cosmological, to give people an image of the universe: what it is made of, what it looks like, and above all who inhabits it. The third function is sociological, telling people how they are supposed to behave, and to support a certain social order. Finally, the fourth function, called the psychological or the pedagogical, is "how to live a human lifetime under any circumstances" (Power 31). With these four functions, we can get an idea of how mythology works. These four functions of myth will continue to appear throughout the present study.

However, there remains one final problem. We have been speaking about the spiritual problem of *modern* people, and part of this discussion has been how the old religions are no longer meaningful or relevant. On the other hand, myth, almost by definition, is *old*, often so old that we do not know how the stories first came into being or who "wrote" them. So even if we accept myth as a teacher, we are still faced with the problem of how to make it relevant today. Maybe Campbell is right when he says that the old forms do not work anymore. If this is true, then what is needed is a *modern myth*.

It is now time to introduce the matter at hand: *The Sandman*, a series of graphic novels by Neil Gaiman, which constitutes what we have already alluded to, a modern myth. At its most simple, *The Sandman* is the story of Morpheus, the King of Dreams, also called "Dream." "The Sandman," another of Dream's names, comes from the children's story of the one who sprinkles sand in their eyes when they are asleep. But he is no fairy tale. He is one of the Endless, a set of seven beings who have ruled the universe since the beginning of time. They are not gods, although the mistake could easily be made. (We will have more to say on gods and how they come to be in their relationship to dreams.) They are more than gods, and existed before the first god was born, and will be around after the last god is dead. Rather, they are manifestations of consciousness, and their names are their functions. They are, from oldest to youngest: Destiny, Death, Dream, Destruction, twins Desire and Despair, and Delirium, who was once Delight. In a sense, they are the reason we have gods, for they are the constituents of consciousness, for in Gaiman's world the gods come from dreams. Our involvement with the Endless begins in 1988, when Dream is freed from a 72-year imprisonment. He returns to find that his realm has decayed in his absence, but also that he has been somehow changed, *tainted*, by his experience. The seventy-six issues of *The Sandman* tell the story of Dream's journey to become human. But more than that, *Sandman* is a story about not just Dream and the Endless, but about stories, about myth. And it is a story about what it means to be human, as Campbell said, how to live a human lifetime.

The first question to be settled, before diving into the material, is what makes *The Sandman* a myth? The minimal definition, stories about gods, certainly applies. After all, the Endless may not technically be gods, but they have godlike powers, and serve the functions of gods. One thing that makes the series mythic is that it draws from worlds of myth; one way to see the series is as a "greatest hits" of world mythology. Before the story is over, the Norse Odin, Loki, and Thor, Jewish and Christian figures Lucifer, Eve, Cain and Abel, the Japanese Susano-no-Moto, the Greek Muse Calliope and her son Orpheus, as well as representatives from Faerie and world folklore, move across the pages, all interacting with the main characters and each other. Gaiman uses mythical figures from many different cultures, underscoring the point that the myths of all cultures are equally valid. Anything that claims to be a modern myth must move beyond the boundaries of individual cultures, and Gaiman does this.

Beyond using elements from past mythology, Gaiman has crafted a myth in which the Endless are the main characters, a myth that works in dialogue with Campbell's four functions. The first function, that of mystical wonder, is perhaps the best represented, as *Sandman* is full of awe and wonder: at the universe, and especially at the human spirit; the use of "mysticism" is not inappropriate here. The second function, cosmology, is again integrative, as the cosmology of the Endless exist behind and in support of the many pantheons of the world's cultures (which by the way are no less real). The third function, the sociological, is perhaps best left for later discussion, except to say that the old ethics of established religions are no longer adequate. Here, we diverge from Campbell; Gaiman's social vision does not validate an established social order but instead critiques it. As a modern myth, *Sandman* addresses people who have been left out of past discourses, those who have been marginalized. Finally, the fourth, psychological function is present not only in the story of Dream, but as a myth, the entire work of *Sandman* can help to move a reader through the stages of life. To do this, we must learn to live *through* a story, in order for the modern myth to work in the same way myths have sustained communities for thousands of years.

The discussion of *The Sandman* as modern myth has of course just begun, but it should be emphasized that the body of the series can be seen not just as incorporating mythic elements, but *as a myth in itself*. Much of this determination comes from Campbell's functions, but it is a notion we will return to. Gaiman distinguishes myth from simple stories in that myth "goes down a long way," and *Sandman* certainly fits this distinction, as the series has tremendous depth. But what ultimately makes these stories so compelling is their humanity. Under the prodigious craft and showmanship of manipulating so many characters and myths lies a very human heart. It is ultimately this quality that makes the series so satisfying, so transformative, and so enduring.

The rest of this discussion, then, will be an examination of the ways *Sandman* serves as a modern myth, a solution to the modern dilemma that has been sketched out. Section One traces the relationship and kinship between myths and dreams. Dreams are very important, and in fact much of *Sandman* takes place in dreams. Section Two deals with the hero myth, that most ubiquitous of mythic elements. *Sandman* can be read as a hero myth, but not without some modifications to the concept, as Dream undertakes a journey from being a structuring principle of the universe to being human. Section Three focuses on the role of death, and of change. Any successful myth has to deal with these facts, and the characters of Death (mortality) and Delirium (change) are central in many places. Section Four centers on the notions of freedom and responsibility, and their role in the series, as questions of responsibility in opposition to freedom, including the freedom to walk away, are important to the story. In addition, I examine the problem of evil in the text. Section Five discusses Gaiman's synthesis of old and new elements in these stories, and lays out a return to polytheism, albeit a changed polytheism, as a possible solution to the modern dilemma. Also, I consider Gaiman's mix of reinterpreting established mythic figures and providing his own framework, the Endless. Gaiman's work also contains elements of folklore, although it is often difficult to separate myth from folklore. And here, *Sandman* also contains a kind of social vision that differs from traditional views: a new way of how to treat each other. Finally, Section Six focuses on myths as stories. The art of storytelling, both oral and written, is an important theme that runs throughout *Sandman*, as the most vital of human activities. The role of the artist in making myth is also an important concept.

In addition, the sections are linked in a journey through the text. Section one serves as an introduction to the world of *The Sandman*, and of myth, and provides a conceptual framework in which to discuss the text. Sections two through four focus on important themes addressed by myth: the role of the hero, mortality and change, freedom and responsibility, and the problem of evil. Sections five and six return explicitly to the idea of the modern myth, by examining the role of old and new elements, with special attention being paid to a new sociology of myth, and the role of the artist and storyteller in creating the myth.

In the end, *The Sandman* is as multifaceted as myth itself, but the theme of myth will tie everything together. Our instinct for the sacred and for religious feeling is alive and well, even if we do not always choose to recognize it. For even when the established religions fail us, there is always hope. In many ways, *The Sandman* is about hope, that most precious of human qualities. Given the problem of the modern age, if we are to live, we need hope. And no matter what, there is always hope.

"DREAM A LITTLE DREAM OF ME . . .": THE RELATIONSHIP OF DREAMS AND MYTH IN CAMPBELL, JUNG, AND GAIMAN'S *SANDMAN*

"A dream is a personal experience of that deep, dark ground that is the support of our conscious lives, and a myth is the society's dream. The myth is the public dream and the dream is the private myth."
—Joseph Campbell

"Dreams are weird and stupid and they scare me."
—Rose Walker

To associate myths and dreams with one another is hardly a new enterprise. Religious traditions going back thousands of years have viewed dreams as a source of knowledge and intuition, and have connected this information with the central narratives of their traditions. If myth is to be seen as a living phenomenon that connects to all aspects of people's lives, then dreams cannot be ignored—after all, we spend a third of our lives in the realm of dreams. Modern psychologists tell us that dreams are essential to mental and physical health, but they are only telling us what we knew all along. Still, in modern times, the connection between myths and dreams has come even more into the fore. In the early twentieth century, doctors began to notice that the dreams and visions of their patients bore a striking resemblance to the motifs and narratives of various religious traditions, traditions with which the patients often had no familiarity. With the advent of Carl Jung's theory of the collective unconscious, a new era of relationship between myth and dream was ushered in. The claim was that not only do myths and dreams share material and patterns, they come from the same place: the human psyche. This theory was developed even further by later scholars, such as Joseph Campbell, who drew analogies between the dreams of an individual, and the myths of a people.

Campbell's theory brings us to the matter at hand: what is the relationship between myth and dream in *The Sandman?* Certainly, this is at least a good place to start, as the series is a myth that in many places is about dreams and how they affect the lives of dreamers. Of course, the connection is even stronger than that. The central character in *Sandman* is Morpheus, the Lord of Dreams. He presides over the Dreaming, the collective realm where dreams do not merely reflect reality; they *are* reality. Simply put, he lives in dreams, and as a constituent of consciousness, he *is* the psychological function of dreaming. Beyond Dream (the character), the structure of *Sandman* reflects the kinship between myths and dreams. The Dreaming is inhabited by characters taken from myth, most notably Eve, Cain, and Abel. The Dreaming itself, I would argue, is a dramatization of Jung's "collective unconscious," making concrete what he perceived in metaphor. Finally, according to both Gaiman and Campbell, the gods themselves come from dreams, and are born and nurtured in dreams (of course, there are also other characters in the Dreaming besides gods). And in *The Sandman*, dreams are respected as their own form of reality. While some theories reductively pigeonhole dreams as reflections of neuroses, in Gaiman's universe, dreams are real, and this fact points to another theme in Gaiman's work, respect for inner realities. It is never "just" a dream. Rather, it is a dream, but dreams have a supreme importance. What better place, then, to start with a series about how myths are made, born, and die, than with an examination of the role of dreams. Thus, we take a ride into dreams. Pay no attention to the man in black.

One of the key principles of the relationship between myths and dreams is that they are somehow connected. Campbell says that "indeed, between the worlds of myth and dream there are many instructive analogies. When we leave the field of our waking lives . . . we descend into a timeless realm of the unconscious" (Transformations 206). He continues, that in dreams, "the logic, the heroes, and the deeds of myth survive into modern times" (Hero with a Thousand Faces, 4). Gaiman takes this idea to the next level, and in doing so makes a pronouncement about the nature of the gods themselves: that gods are in fact magnified dreams. With a psychological interpretation of myths, such as that used by Campbell and Jung, saying "the gods" does not refer to some outer reality, but to an inner one. Campbell says "the archetypes of mythology (God, angels, incarnations, and so forth) . . . are of the mind" (Masks 583). He also refers to the transformative power of religion as leading "not into outer space but into inward space, to the place from which all being comes, into the consciousness that is the source of all things, the kingdom of heaven within" (Power 56). In a similar vein, the gods become metaphors of inner "potentialities;" thus, myth, at its heart, is about people, and their inner worlds. Campbell asks, "What is a god? A god is a personification of a motivating power or a value system that functions in human life and the universe—the powers of your own body and of nature. The myths are metaphorical of spiritual potentiality in the human being, and the same powers that animate our life animate the life of the world" (Power 22). Thus, myths are metaphorical of a deeper truth. Elsewhere, Campbell states that "gods are all metaphors of this ultimate mystery, the mystery of your own being" (Transformations 155). Beyond the fact that the gods are metaphors lies a second point, that gods are only as valid in that they reflect some aspect of our being. We care about gods not because they control fire or water or lightning, but because they are a part of us. Campbell also says that "all the gods are within: within you—within the world" (Masks 650). Put another way, "the source of the gods is in your own heart" (Hero's Journey 128). Thus, ultimately, myths are about *us*. And the realization of this fact is an important step for more than one character in *Sandman*. Of course, although dreams and myth are related, there are important differences between them, as we will see.

With this shift, from gods as physical beings to gods as metaphors of aspects of ourselves, the relationship of myth to dream comes into focus. Just as gods can function as symbols, so can elements from our dreams. The next step, then, is to identify the gods with dreams. Campbell says that "all the gods, all the heavens, all the worlds, are within us. They are magnified dreams, and dreams are manifestations in image form of the energies of the body in conflict with each other. That is what myth is. Myth is a manifestation in symbolic images, in metaphorical images, of the energies of the organs in conflict with each other" (Power 39). Then, he states that "the myth is the public dream and the dream is the private myth" (40). Elsewhere, he says "Dream is the personalized myth, myth the depersonalized dream; both myth and dream are symbolic in the same general way of the dynamics of the psyche" (Campbell, Hero with a Thousand Faces, 19). At this point, if we are to accept Campbell's psychological reading of myth, the relationship between myth and dream seems well-established.

In the *Power of Myth* videos, Campbell also says that "myths and dreams come from the same place" (Tape 1). Of course, exactly what that "place" is may be a matter of debate. For Campbell (as for Jung) it was the unconscious, or at least the psyche. For Gaiman, it is the Dreaming. From Campbell's discussion, the most important concept in relation to *The Sandman* is that of gods as magnified dreams. At first glance, however, such a reading might seem as reductive as those against which Campbell rails. After all, if the gods are all metaphors, then they do not *really* exist. However, with *The Sandman*, we are dealing with a myth, a work of art, in which such beings can exist without our having to worry about whether or not they exist in the real world. In fact, one of the lessons of *Sandman* is that inner, imaginary worlds are just as real and valid as the solid, "real" world, and that each one of us has not just one inner world, but many.

Returning to Campbell, then, the flip-side of the gods' status as metaphors and magnified dreams, (the other side of the coin, if you will) is what happens after the gods have left the realm of dreams. In Gaiman's work, this stage is eloquently described by Ishtar, once Astarte, a goddess, now working in a seedy strip club, just before she goes off to her death: "I know how gods begin, Roger. We start as dreams. Then we walk out of dreams into the land. We are worshipped and loved, and take power to ourselves. And then one day there's no one left to worship us. And in the end, each little god and goddess takes its last journey back into dreams . . . And what comes after, not even *we* know" (Sandman 45:20). This quotation is filled with implications. First, of course, is the association of gods with dreams. Gods and goddesses start their journey in dreams. From one dreamer, they can spread to others, until an entire people believes in them. And one day, after being nurtured in dreams, they step out into the world, becoming gods in their own right. The immediate implication of this journey is to confirm Campbell's notion of gods as magnified dreams. However, Gaiman's treatment of the subject also runs much deeper. One implication of this is that gods, often said to be immortal, are in fact very mortal. They depend on people's worship for their very lives. *Sandman* is full of stories of gods who have been forced to deal with the loss of worship. For some, their time has passed, while for others, the modern "demythologization" has taken its toll. And without worship, they will die. The character Death, at one point, tells us that this process takes a while, but it is bound to happen, as "Mythologies take longer to die than people believe. They linger on in a kind of dream country" (Sandman 20:21). This "dream country" is the province of the Sandman. And while religious traditions are filled with accounts of the gods "needing" the sacrifices that people make to them, nowhere else is the gods' dependence identified with belief to the degree that it is in *Sandman*. And this need for belief works in both directions. Just as gods need us, so do we have a need to believe in them.

As Destruction tells us, there is no such thing as a one-sided coin. And the flip-side to the gods' needing people for worship is that we need them just as much. Frank McConnell, in his preface to the *Sandman Book of Dreams*, asks the question, "How do gods die? And when they do, what happens to them *then*? You might as well ask, how do gods get born? All three questions are, really, the same question. And they all have a common assumption: *that humankind can no more live without gods than you can kill yourself by holding your breath*" (2, emphasis mine). Just as gods need us, so do we need them. Since the time of the Enlightenment, people have moved further and further into secularization. If we take Freud as the high-water mark of demythization and post-Enlightenment positivism, then his *Future of an Illusion* epitomizes the already existing argument that religious belief is, in fact, an illusion, and an illusion that mankind can and will (even must) learn to live without. However, we now stand almost a century later, and whether the loss of religious belief has truly helped us is a dubious claim indeed. In other words, we have killed the gods, and are only now beginning to wonder whether doing so was a good idea. For many, the loss of religion has meant the loss of meaning and purpose in life.

Like others, Gaiman understands this situation, what has been called "the spiritual problem of modern humans." Destruction's formulation of this problem led him to abandon his realm (albeit for slightly different reasons—see part 4). Still, the point here is not simply that the increasing march toward rationality has taken a toll in our spiritual lives. It is that people who think they are living in a world without God (or gods) are really just fooling themselves. If the old gods are lost, we will simply invent new ones. The central point here is the importance of *belief*. It is belief that is central to keeping gods alive, and it is belief that is equally important for people. McConnell continues his discussion, that "We need gods . . . not so much to worship or sacrifice to, but because they satisfy our need—distinctive from that of all the other animals—to imagine a meaning, a sense to our lives, to satisfy our hunger to believe that the muck and chaos of daily existence does, after all *tend* somewhere" (Preface 2). This kind of belief is born of a need for meaning, and it powers the "gods as magnified dreams" dynamic. And this sense of meaning is what makes life worth living.

The second major point in the relationship between myths and dreams lies in the psychological background of both. This background, quite literally, is Carl Jung's idea of the "collective unconscious," which shows a strong kinship with Gaiman's "Dreaming." It is from the collective unconscious that both myths and dreams spring. According to Jung, this layer of the unconscious is "not individual but universal," and "more or less the same in all individuals" (Jung, Archetypes 3-4). Jung agrees with Campbell, that gods and heroes "[dwell] nowhere except in the soul of man," and that "the psyche contains all the images that have ever given rise to myths" (Archetypes 6-7). It is this part of the psyche that is the source of the images and sto-ries that so captivate us. According to Jung, the collective uncon-scious is inherited biologically, "[owing its] existence exclusively to heredity" (42). And although the collective unconscious is the source for myths as well, it is dreams that are the "main source" of knowledge about it—being unconscious, dreams are "pure products of nature not falsified by any conscious purpose" (Jung, Archetypes 48). Thus, this layer of the psyche is passed down through the generations biologically, and is the result of the same process of evolution that produced our other forms of in-stinctive behavior.

The second major point about the collective unconscious, af-ter its residency in the psyche, is that it is the same in all people. Jung says that "from the unconscious there emanate determin-ing influences which, independently of tradition, guarantee in every single individual a similarity and even a sameness of expe-rience, and also of the way it is represented imaginatively. One of the main proofs of this is the almost universal parallelism be-tween mythological motifs, which, on account of their quality as primordial images, I have called *archetypes*" (Archetypes 58). Under this scheme, the archetypes are the inner psychic images that we form instinctively, and which are the precursors of the religious and mythological images we create. Although I am not qualified to address the veracity of this claim, it might well be that, as other theorists do, Jung overestimated the similarities between mythic traditions and ignored their differences, as some critics have claimed. Still, it is important to note that Jung is not saying that all mythologies are the same. Archetypes are not the images of myth themselves; "it is not, therefore, a question of in-herited *ideas*, but of inherited *possibilities* of ideas" (Jung, Ar-chetypes 66).

Elsewhere, Jung calls the archetypes "primordial," at least as old as the human species. He also says that "they are the 'hu-man quality' of the human being, and the specifically human form his activities take" (Archetypes 78), thus forming one of the things that define us. He claims "the true history of the mind is not preserved in learned volumes but in the living mental organ-ism of everyone" (Psychology and Religion 41). It is difficult to overestimate the importance of these phenomena; Jung says, "I am of the opinion that the psyche is the most tremendous fact of human life" (Archetypes 116). He also says that "psyche is existent, even existence itself" (Psychology and Religion 12). Elsewhere, Jung lays out the psyche as consisting of both the conscious mind and "an indefinitely large hinterland of unconscious psyche" (Psychology and Religion 47). Finally, Campbell has commented on Jung's ideas, as he was influenced by them as well; "The psyche is the inward experience of the human body, which is essentially the same in all human beings . . . Out of this common ground have come what Jung has called the archetypes, which are the common idea of myths" (Campbell, Power 51). Here, we have an etiological explanation for Campbell's statement that dreams and myths come from the same place; that place is the collective unconscious. And although dreams and myths have important differences, they are inextricably linked.

In another work, *Modern Man in Search of a Soul*, Jung discusses the collective unconscious further. In particular, the production of dreams is important, as "dreams may give expression to ineluctable truths, to philosophical pronouncements, illusions, wild fantasies, memories, [etc] . . . One thing we ought never to forget: almost half of our lives is passed in a more or less unconscious state" (Modern Man 11). In arguing for the importance of the unconscious, he says "When we see that at least a half of man's life is passed in this realm, that consciousness has its roots there, and that the unconscious operates in and out of waking existence, it would seem incumbent upon medical psychology to sharpen its perceptions by a systematic study of dreams. No one doubts the importance of conscious experience; why then should we question the importance of unconscious happenings?" (15). Later, he tells us that "the collective unconscious, moreover, seems not to be a person, but something like an unceasing stream or perhaps an ocean of images and figures which drift into consciousness in our dreams . . ." (Modern Man 186). And connected with dreams, always, is myth, and while this connection was made more forcefully by later theorists like Campbell, Jung still makes the connection, as "myth for Jung *is* the naked expression of the unconscious" (Segal, Jung on Mythology 25-6). At one point, Campbell quotes Jung as saying "the typical motifs in dreams . . . permit a comparison with the motifs of mythology" (Masks 644). Jung also says that "man has, everywhere and always, spontaneously developed religious forms of expression, and that the human psyche from time immemorial has been shot through with religious ideas. Whoever cannot see this aspect of the human psyche is blind" (Modern Man 122). Commenting on this idea, Anne Ulanov says that "operating in us, independent of our will, [the religious instinct] is a capacity for and urge toward conscious relationship to transpersonal deity" (18). The idea of the psyche as being naturally religious also opens a dialogue between Jung and scholars of religion.

While some depth psychologists have tried to explain religion away as a relic of a past age, and to envision myth as a "quaint" but outmoded system of belief, Jung saw religious experience as an integral part of psychic life, and began to study religion in order to more fully understand the psyche. In *Psychology and Religion*, he calls religion "one of the earliest and most universal activities of the human mind" (1). In particular, Jung focuses on what Rudolf Otto calls the "numinosum," which Jung defines as "a dynamic existence or affect, not caused by an arbitrary act of will" (4). In light of this, he defines religion as "the term that designates the attitude peculiar to a consciousness which has been altered by the experience of the numinosum" (Psychology 6). Anne Ulanov comments on Jung's interest in religion, that he "valued the numinous above all, and he conceived of health as finding life's meaning" (Ulanov 1). Ulanov also sees the need to "humanize archetypal symbols into livable forms in our ordinary lives" (2). As we will see, one of the ways of looking at *Sandman* is as a story of the humanization of myth. Again speaking of Jung's impact on religion, Ulanov says that he "works to reconnect religion to its archaic instinctive roots, from which the symbols of theology and ritual spring. When we reach and link ourselves to the primordial religious experience deep within us . . . Religion ceases to be merely an intellectual activity or a systematic exploration of abstract principles of being. *Instead, it reaches into our hearts, our souls, our bowels*" (23, emphasis mine). It is exactly this immediacy of experience that is missing in many people's lives today. Thus, while he wrote in the field of psychology, Jung was intensely interested in religious experience. It is perhaps his greatest expression of humanity's religious impulse that Jung says "one could almost say that if all the world's traditions were cut off at a single blow, the whole of mythology and the whole history of religion would start over again with the next generation" (Jung on Mythology 211). Under this scheme, it is indeed appropriate to speak of a religious *instinct*. Asking these kinds of religious questions is as much a part of what it means to be human as anything else.

Having established the relevance of Jung and his theory of the collective unconscious to religion, we can look at these ideas' relevance to *The Sandman*. First and most apparent is Gaiman's formulation of "the Dreaming," Morpheus's realm. Essentially, the Dreaming is a place that contains everything that has ever been dreamed or that has been produced in dreams. As Campbell says about dreams, "it is the realm we enter in sleep. We carry it within ourselves forever . . . All the life-potentialities that we never managed to bring to adult realization, those other portions of oneself, are there; for such golden seeds do not die" (Hero with a Thousand Faces 17). Everything is there, and more than once Dream moves between people's dreams, taking items as he needs them, or moving through them to where he needs to go (Sandman 1:31 and 5:18, respectively). It is in dreams that Dream's power is paramount, and he has the power to influence them, even as they happen to people.

Another example of the collective unconscious in *Sandman* is Lucien's library. The library, maintained by Lucien, one of Dream's most conscientious helpers, is unusual indeed, as "somewhere in here is every story that has ever been dreamed," including stories that were only finished or written in dreams (Sandman 22:2). Elsewhere, Lucien says "the library of Dream is the largest library there never was" (Vertigo Jam 2). It contains "every book that's ever been dreamed. Every book that's ever been imagined. Every book that's ever been lost" (Sandman 57:12). One major divergence between Jung's theory and the Dreaming might be that dreams are (for Jung) to a large extent unstructured, while the Dreaming is somewhat ordered (at least the parts inhabited by Dream). There are other areas of the Dreaming, however: lands and skerries that operate largely without Dream's control (one example being the land in "A Game of You"). Still, this difference could be attributed to a small scope of vision. At best, in our dreams, we only manage to experience aspects of Dream, and of the Dreaming. But if we were able to see both in a more systematic manner (as we do when we read *Sandman*), then perhaps our vision would look more like Gaiman's vision. Still, it seems that at least a rough approximation can be made that "the Dreaming" is essentially the same as Jung's collective unconscious, or at least an artist's interpretation of it. The rest comes rather quickly. If we know that there are certain images and motifs that are embedded in our consciousness, then what would happen if they existed with some systematicity or purpose? It might look like the Dreaming.

Another point of dialogue between Jung's theory and *The Sandman* is the presence of archetypes in the Dreaming. If the archetypes are the way in which the collective unconscious expresses itself, and the Dreaming is the collective unconscious, then one would expect to find the archetypes in the Dreaming. And, in fact, many archetypes do "live" in the Dreaming. Cain and Abel, the first pair of brothers, live next to each other as the keepers of the houses of mysteries and secrets, respectively. And in typical archetypal form, the pair act out the primordial fratricidal killing over and over again (Sandman 2:15). After being killed by Cain, Abel revives, picks himself up, and continues with his duties (Sandman 2:22). Moreover, the archetypes of brothers in conflict and fratricide, represented by Cain and Abel, are revealed to go back even farther than the Jewish and Christian Biblical story we know today. In "A Parliament of Rooks," Abel reveals that when they came to inhabit the Dreaming, they lived in another world, and did not look even remotely human (Sandman 40:21). This and other passages have led to a mini-controversy among Gaiman's readers. Some have supposed that Gaiman privileges Jewish and Christian mythologies over other systems. Gaiman, however, denies this. The figures these readers point to—Eve, Cain, and Abel among them—are, for Gaiman, part of a pattern much older than the Bible. Eve, who lives in a cave on the borders of nightmare, is there less as the Biblical Eve than as the archetypal mother, and as an expression of the archetypal female, as when the Furies (or the Kindly Ones) visit the Dreaming, they do not attack Eve because "she is an aspect of ourselves" (Sandman 65:14). This is not to say that the characters do not borrow aspects of the Biblical accounts; one of the joys of reading *Sandman* is to watch Gaiman interweaving different mythologies. Essentially, all the myths are true, in one form or another, in that they coexist in the world of *Sandman.* Other "archetypal" but less famous characters include the Corinthian (nightmare par excellence), Brute and Glob (force and cunning), Fiddler's Green (who is somewhere between a person and a place) and Mervyn Pumkinhead, the comic relief of the Dreaming. And of course, many other gods and archetypal figures may not live in the Dreaming, but visit there, as in the case of "A Season of Mists," or Odin in "The Kindly Ones."

After familiarizing ourselves with Jung's ideas concerning the psyche, Campbell's formulations make more sense. Just as the psyche contains a hidden level behind the conscious mind, so Campbell interprets myth as establishing an invisible plane of support for our lives in the world, as "I would say that is the basic theme of all mythology—that there is an invisible plane supporting the visible one" (Power 71). Also, he says that "there are dimensions of your being and a potential for realization and consciousness that are not included in your concept of yourself. Your life is much deeper and broader than you conceive it to be here" (Power 58). Similarly, in *Sandman*, at the end of "The Doll's House," Rose Walker writes that "If my dream was true, then everything we know, everything we think we know is a lie. It means the world's about as solid and as reliable as a layer of scum on the top of a well of black water that goes down forever, and there are things in the depths that I don't even want to think about. It means more than that. It means we're just dolls. We don't have a clue what's really going down, we just kid ourselves that we're in control of our lives" (Sandman 16:17-8).

What Rose is grappling with is the idea that the world has hidden depths, very similar to Campbell's "invisible plane of support." Still, Rose also comes face to face with the fact that pure, unadulterated religious experience can be scary as hell. She finds it in herself to regain hope and move on with her life. Campbell also speaks of mythology as going "down and down and down" (Power 39). The theme of hidden depths runs throughout the series.

And at the same time Rose uses the metaphor of the Doll's House to describe the influence of unseen archetypal forces, Dream makes a similar claim about the gods, or even the Endless themselves, being influenced by men and women. As he tells Desire, "We the Endless are the servants of the living—we are not their masters. We exist because they know, deep in their hearts, that we exist. When the last living thing has left the universe, then our task will be done. And we do not manipulate them. If anything, they manipulate us. We are their toys. Their dolls, if you will" (Sandman 16:22). Here, we have, perfectly balanced against Rose's claims of powerlessness in the face of the gods, a contrasting assessment from Dream, that the gods and even the Endless exist because people *know* they exist. Thus, not only the world, but individual people too have hidden depths to them. Here, we connect with the earlier formulation of the gods' owing their existence to belief on the part of the people who worship them. Without the belief of humans, the gods wither and die. And again, we have the mutual dependence between deities and people, a dependence that is mediated by inner worlds. The concept of inner worlds also surfaces at the end of "A Game of You," as the positive, inner side to Rose's lament. Barbie says at Wanda's grave, "Everybody has a secret world inside of them. I mean everybody. All of the people in the whole world—no matter how dull and boring they are on the outside. Inside them they've all got unimaginable, magnificent, wonderful, stupid, amazing worlds . . . Not just one world. Hundreds of them. Thousands, maybe" (Sandman 37:19). This means that no matter how people appear, they all have unexplored, hidden depths inside them . . . secret worlds.

Finally, just as myth and dream are linked, and just as we

have seen "the power of myth" (from Campbell), so in *Sandman* we see the power of dreams. One example of this is the "Dream of a Thousand Cats." In it, we are told the tale that cats were once the dominant species on earth, but that one day the humans rose up, as a leader said, "Dream! Dreams shape the world. Dreams create the world anew, every night" (Sandman 18:17). The humans began to dream of a world in which *they* were the dominant species, and when enough of them (say, 1000) did so, they changed the world. However, they did more than change the world as it was. Dream (as a cat) tells a cat leader that "they dreamed the world so it always was the way it is now . . . There never was a world of high cat-ladies and cat-lords. They changed the universe from the beginning of all things, until the end of time" (Sandman 18:19). The issue ends with the cat urging her fellow cats to join together and dream of the world in which they were the lords of it. And although one cat doubts whether you could get a thousand cats to do anything together, the fact remains: dreams have the power to change and shape the world. In theory, there is no telling how many times this has happened, as each time it occurs, the world is changed so that it always was the way it is now. This shows the tremendous power of dreams, as they can recreate the entire world. Here, we see an example of Gaiman's statement that the business of fantasy is to make metaphors concrete. In this case, dreams literally change the world. Further, from this principle, we can accept any number of alternate worlds and histories, places in which things happened differently. Such a system is hinted at in "The Golden Boy," as different Americas are mentioned according to who was elected president, but the possibilities for dreams to change the world are endless. Put another way, the world we know is but one of many, or even infinite worlds.

Also, there is the episode in which Dream goes to Hell in search of his stolen helmet. After he regains it, Lucifer threatens not to let him leave, and asks what power dreams have in Hell. Dream responds "ask yourselves, all of you . . . What power would Hell have if those here imprisoned were not able to dream of Heaven?" (Sandman 4:22). The demons are unable to meet his challenge, and he leaves unscathed. Thus, even in Hell, dreams have power, and as in "A Dream of a Thousand Cats," they can change worlds.

Finally, one last qualification must be made concerning the relationship between myths and dreams. Although many useful parallels can be drawn between the two, there are key differences between the two classes of phenomena. Campbell says that "we must note that myths are not exactly comparable to dream. Their figures originate from the same sources—the unconscious wells of fantasy . . . but [myths] are not the spontaneous products of sleep. On the contrary, their patterns are consciously controlled" (Hero with a Thousand Faces 256). Likewise, Jung says that "strictly speaking, a myth is a historical document. It is told, it is recorded, but it is not itself a dream. It is the product of an unconscious process in a particular social group, at a particular time, at a particular place" (Jung on Mythology 107). While myths are consciously shaped and created, dreams are the raw product of the unconscious mind. Analogous to the split between dream and myth, Gaiman speaks about the difference between "dream-logic" and "story-logic," as the contents of a dream often do not translate to making a good story. With dreams, "for you it was interesting and fascinating; but it's not a story. And dreams very, very rarely contain stories; but they will contain images" that you can pull up from the depths (Sound & Spirit interview). Thus, crafting stories (or myths) is a very different process than dreaming. It is easy to overlook in one's enthusiasm that dreams and myth are not identical; however, similarities do exist, and both are rich worlds into which we can delve.

At this point, the kinship between dreams and myths should be apparent. Both spring from the biologically-ingrained collective unconscious, and "live" in what Jung called the "vast hinterland of the psyche." In addition, gods can be seen as magnified dreams, as has been pointed out by both Campbell and Gaiman, revealing a two-way process, in which people need to believe in *something* to bring meaning to their lives, and gods need people to believe in them in order to survive. On both sides, belief is the key step. The Dreaming can be seen as an approximation of the collective unconscious, and it not only contains many archetypal figures, but also reveals a hidden plane of existence behind the visible one. We spend a third of our lives in Morpheus's realm, and dreams, whether true dreams or waking dreams, have the power to change the world.

Given the relationship between myths and dreams, it makes sense that a modern myth, one that recognizes the "inner" religious life, should be concerned with dreams. By setting so much of *The Sandman* in dreams, Gaiman is able to weave his own myth with characters from the full body of world mythology. Jung says that the modern gods "are as powerful and as awe-inspiring as ever, in spite of their new disguise- the so-called psychical functions" (Psychology 102). Of course, the formulation of "new" gods coincides exactly with the Endless, who are manifestations of consciousness. What Gaiman adds, though, is that the Endless are so much more than gods; they provide the background and the secret cause by which the gods exist. Gaiman then crafts a new mythology around the existing mythologies. And, as with the older myths, dreams are key in shaping these mythic narratives. We will return later to what exactly is meant by "myth." In terms of an overall study, Gaiman's use of the Endless and incorporation of many mythologies constitutes what Campbell calls the cosmological function of myth. And the important lesson to take from this discussion is that the myths (and dreams) are *real*.

HUMANIZATION, CHANGE, AND REBIRTH: THE HERO'S JOURNEY IN *SANDMAN*

"Furthermore, we have not even to risk the adventure alone; for the heroes of all time have gone before us; the labyrinth is thoroughly known; we have only to follow the thread of the hero-path."

—Joseph Campbell

"Look. Boss. I'm not sure I'm going to get another chance to say this or . . . hell. You know what I mean. So. Whatever happens. It was good being your raven. Really. I mean . . . It was good being your friend."

—Matthew the Raven

Perhaps the most widespread, and the most enduring, type of myth is the hero myth. An individual or a god, armed with special abilities, embarks on a journey, faces tests of mettle and determination, slays terrible monsters, comes to a mystical realization, and returns to the world of men with a boon for society, or is transfigured and joins the gods. In fact, the stories are so varied and widespread that no single formula can contain them all. Still, when we speak of a hero, most people will know what we're talking about. Joseph Campbell devoted his first major work, *The Hero with a Thousand Faces*, to analyzing the hero myth, and it has been said that tales of heroes are among the easiest to classify within the sphere of mythology. David Adams Leeming even goes so far as to suggest that "the quest myth in one sense is the *only* myth—that is, all other myths are part of the quest myth . . . Psychologically all heroes, as we have seen, represent humankind's search for the self" (152).

But the pattern does not stop there. Not only the old texts of mythology, but also the modern world of television, novels, and especially the cinema is filled with the exploits of more-than-mere-men. The role that was filled two generations ago by the likes of Douglas Fairbanks, a generation past by John Wayne and the Lone Ranger, has taken on a kaleidoscope of personae in the present day: Mark Hamill, Carrie Fisher, and Harrison Ford in the "Star Wars" saga, Ford again as Indiana Jones, and (lest we go all sexist) Buffy the Vampire Slayer, the street fighter Chun LI, Angela Bassett in "Strange Days," and FBI Agent Dana Scully. And then, of course, there is the superhero. Dating back to the "Golden Age" of comics in the 40's and 50's, our culture is filled with depictions of costumed heroes with magical powers saving the day from a bunch of equally super-powered villains. Of course, sometimes the heroic journey is an inward one, in which the hero comes to some deeper realization or enlightenment (here one thinks of the story of the Buddha). In this way, it might even be said that any tale of achievement is a hero tale. In these stories, we come to identify with the great powers of the hero, as "the ordinary man is gripped, freed from his impotence and misery, and raised to an almost super-human status, at least for the time being, and often enough he is sustained by such a conviction for a long time" (Jung On Mythology 95). And since the pattern is so prevalent (especially in comics), a good place to start in examining *The Sandman* might be to ask whether or not it is a hero myth. After all, the hero myth is one of the classic patterns in mythology.

The question of whether *Sandman* is a hero myth is a complex one. Dream is closer to a god than a man, there is no denying his more-than-any-human powers, or his travels into strange and mystical worlds. However, there is more to *The Sandman* than that, and part of the reason why it is may lie in the medium of comics. In comics, the vast majority of the top-selling titles are superhero series, tales that either follow directly or are just a minor tweak away from the hero saga. And while these titles do not lack in archetypal background (as many do draw on myth or literature), what most of them lack is a sense of subtlety. The hero is always valiant, the girl beautiful, and the villain nasty, and the monsters frightful. After forty or fifty years of this, while some exceptional writers (Frank Miller, Alan Moore, J. Michael Straczynski, etc.) continue to produce intelligent, innovative superhero work, the formula is bound to grow stale, and what is needed is someone to prove that the medium is capable of "more than this." One such writer, of course, is Neil Gaiman. While Dream does embark on strange journeys, what really matters is what he has learned, and how he has changed. And the most important change of all, indeed the central plot-line of *Sandman*, is Dream's process of becoming human, following his seventy years of captivity. Rather than a human hero becoming godlike and performing various exploits, Dream starts as more than any god, and over the course of the series, becomes a man. And this process of humanization turns the hero myth on its head. While heroes are typically judged by their exploits (and it is important to remember that not all hero myths focus on the physical), Dream's story is remarkable for his transformation into a human—thus, heroes matter not because they are heroic, but because they are *us*. In this way, the hero myth can be applied to *Sandman* only if it is first enlarged, and the model inverted. That is what I mean when I say that *Sandman* is in its own way a hero myth, but that it provides a new paradigm for hero myths, of an otherworldly being recognizing his essential humanity. In addition, from other characters in the series, we learn that relationality and compassion are critical parts of what we call "being human."

From looking at the issues of *Sandman* that take place before his captivity, one can get a sense of just how far Dream eventually comes. Early on, he is not even remotely human. In "Tales in the Sand" (issue 9, taking place over 10,000 years in the past), he condemns Nada to hell because she refuses to stay with him when she finds out that he is one of the Endless. (Of course, she is right; there is a rule against a human loving one of the Endless, but no matter.) And perhaps most significant is his behavior during the Orpheus episode. After Orpheus's beloved Eurydice dies, Dream advises his son, "it is the mortal way. You attend the funeral, you bid the dead farewell. You grieve, then you continue with your life. And at times the fact of her absence will hit you like a blow to the chest, and you will weep. But this will happen less and less as time goes on. She is dead. You are alive. So live" (Orpheus 15). The advice is sound, but it is also cold. And Dream refuses to help when Orpheus wants to go off to regain Eurydice. After Orpheus is torn apart by the Baccants (and is still alive due to Death's promise not to take him), Dream sees him one last time, as saying goodbye "Seemed the proper thing to do" (Orpheus 47). When Orpheus calls him "father," he responds "'Father?' Did you not say you were no longer my son?" (48). Not being one to forgive a slight, he tells his son "Your life is your own, Orpheus. Your death, likewise. Always, and forever, your own. Fare well. We shall not meet again" (48). The priesthood Dream establishes takes care of Orpheus' head, but he can never die. Dream has in effect condemned his son to eternal life, when he wants nothing more than to die and be reunited with Eurydice. Later, when Orpheus' head is stolen, Dream works through an intermediary, because he cannot be seen intervening in the matter (Sandman 29:16). In the cases of Nada and Orpheus lie two episodes for which Dream will eventually try to atone, and which will in the end cost him his life. One might wonder how a man could act this way, especially towards his son, but therein lies the answer: he is not a man. As we will see, most of the Endless are not even remotely human (except for Death and Destruction).

Still, even the "old" Dream has moments of insight, as is the case in his dealings with Shakespeare. In asking for *The Tempest*, Dream explains his motivation: "I wanted a tale of graceful ends. I wanted a play about a king who drowns his books, and breaks his staff, and leaves his kingdom. About a magician who becomes a man. About a man who turns his back on magic" (Sandman 75:180). He tells Will that he wanted the play because "I will never leave my island." When Shakespeare answers that all men can change, Dream replies: "I am not a man. And I do not change. I asked you earlier if you saw yourself reflected in your tale. I do not. I may not. I am Prince of Stories, Will; but I have no story of my own. Nor shall I ever" (Sandman 75: 182). Dream's response is one of the central ironies in the series, but it is worth noting that this is probably the closest the old (pre-imprisonment) Dream comes to realizing the problem in his life, the lack of humanity. The episode is recounted in the 75th and final issue of *Sandman*, and it truly belongs there, but examined here, it shows that even before his imprisonment, Dream has some moments of insight. And the process of the "magician becoming a man" described here essentially *is* the plot of *The Sandman*, writ large.

The catalytic event that sets Dream on the path to redemption is his capture and imprisonment for seventy-two years in a glass cage by Roderick Burgess, and it is this event that sets the stage for the rest of the series. Gaiman says, "his seventy-two years of imprisonment changed him a great deal; more than he ever realized or understood. He was almost a different entity by the time he emerged from Burgess's glass cage" (Bender 209-210). Although it takes Dream a while to realize he's changed, this change can be seen in "Men of Good Fortune," the interlude story in "The Doll's House," of Dream's once-a-century meeting with Hob Gadling, the mortal who will not die. When Hob calls him lonely in their 1889 meeting, Dream storms out in a huff, and Hob calls after him that if he shows up in 100 years, it will only be because they are friends. It is likely that, had he not been imprisoned, the old, stuffy Dream would not have gone to see Gadling again. But as it happened, Dream shows up and says, "I have always heard it was impolite to keep one's friends waiting. Would you like a drink?" (Sandman 13:24). Somewhere along the way, Dream learned the meaning of friendship.

Still, he has a long way to go, as can be seen by his treatment of Lyta Hall elsewhere in "The Doll's House." After taking apart the dreamworld inhabited by Lyta and her dead husband, and returning him to the land of the dead, he tells Lyta that her unborn child is "his" (Dream's—as it gestated in dreams), and that he would one day return for it (Sandman 12:23). He tells Lyta that he will do "nothing" to her, though (as she points out) he has destroyed her life. While Dream is technically correct (the dreamworld that Hector and Lyta inhabited was created by the nightmares Brute and Glob in Dream's absence and should never have happened), his coldness towards Lyta is telling—and it will come back to haunt him later, as it causes her to go after him when Daniel is kidnapped, setting in motion the events that lead to Dream's demise in "The Kindly Ones."

Another telling episode in Dream's humanization is his decision to come to Calliope's aid when she is imprisoned. After he helps her, she tells him "You have changed, Oneiros. In the old days you would have left me to rot forever, without turning a hair." (Sandman 17:23). Dream responds, "No. I no longer hate you, Calliope. I have learned much in recent times, and . . . no matter. I do not hate you, child." Still he tells Calliope that he does not wish to see her again. He has come a long way, but he has not yet shed all of his old ways. Yet one of the beauties of *Sandman* is seeing the small victories. Another such event co- mes in "A Game of You," when Nuala tells him that she tried to warn Barbie of what was going to happen. Dream thanks her for telling him, then begins to walk off. But he stops, turns around, and tells her she did the right thing. The sequence ends with him walking away and her smiling. The progress Dream is making is tangible, as the human thing to do is to try to relate to Nuala, but it still does not occur to him right away. At this point, we can identify one of the hallmarks of humanity to be relationality, the need for companionship and relationships with others.

The next major step in Dream's humanization comes in "A Season of Mists." At a meeting of the Endless, Desire needles him about Nada, and Death, for once, agrees with Desire; "Con- demning her to an eternity in Hell, just because she turned you down . . . that's a really shitty thing to do" (Sandman 21:22). It is important to note that before this, it does not even occur to Dream that he had acted wrongly towards Nada. And after he frees her, the best he can muster by way of an apology is: "I now think . . . I think I may have acted wrongly. I think perhaps I should apologize. I should tell you that I am sorry" (Sandman 28:5). After Nada becomes angry, Dream acknowledges that there is nothing he can do to make what he did right. Nada eventually accepts his apology, but Dream is left with the knowledge of what he did.

The climax to the whole series comes in "Brief Lives." First, when there is a fire in the hotel, Dream feels responsible for the mortal Ruby's death, and he tells Delirium "We failed her" (Sandman 44:24). In the past, his response would have been more like Pharamond's (Ruby's employer and a god), when he says, "Ruby's dead? Ah me. That's the trouble with mortals. They do that. Not to worry, eh?" (Sandman 46:8). Dream is beginning to realize that the lives of mortals, brief as they are, do matter, and are in fact quite important, since (as we established in the previous section) it is human belief that creates the gods and the Endless. Dream's sense of responsibility (for Ruby's death) compels him to continue his quest, for to stop would mean that Ruby died for nothing.

Later in "Brief Lives.",, the plot centers around Orpheus. In Destiny's garden, the thought of going to see Orpheus occurs to Dream, it overpowers him, and he collapses (47:11-2). Before he goes in to see his son, he says to Delirium, "I have . . . no desire to do this, my sister" (47:18), to which she replies, "I know. I'm sorry." Dream goes on, knowing that asking Orpheus to find Destruction will cause him to ask for a boon, and what that boon will be. When he returns to kill his son, Orpheus tells him "You have changed, since the old days," a statement Dream denies (Sandman 49:3). Still, for the reader, that much is clear. He does Orpheus the merciful deed, killing him, giving him the death he has craved for thousands of years. When he returns to his castle in the Dreaming, he has changed so much that his door guardians do not recognize him. When they ask whether it is him, he tells them "Have I ever told you how much I appreciate your service? That I value you all most highly?" leading one of them to ask, "Is he all right?" (Sandman 49:13).

From the moment Dream kills Orpheus, the rest of *The Sandman* is set, as he has spilled family blood. Frank McConnell, in his introduction to "The Kindly Ones," says that Dream "has killed his son, Orpheus: at Orpheus's request, to be sure, but nevertheless he has killed him. And with that act Dream has entered time, choice, guilt, and regret—has entered the sphere of the human." In "The Kindly Ones," the Dream we see is filled with regret, for his long life, his misdeeds and loneliness, and is so tired. And if we are to view him as human at this point, he is still not comfortable in this new role. Because of this, he often speaks in cryptic asides, as in his interaction with his door guardians, or with his estranged wife Calliope, or when he goes to see Hob Gadling without really knowing why (59:16). It is also interesting to note that by "The Kindly Ones," he cares when other people (Odin, Fiddler's Green) are disappointed in him.

The central moment of revelation comes when Nuala calls on Dream. He tells her that "the ladies [The Furies] have power to avenge blood-crimes . . . And I killed my son. I killed him twice. Once, long ago, when I would not help him; and once . . . more recently . . . when I did. The ladies are empowered to hound those who spill family blood. I have Orpheus's blood on my hands, Nuala. I killed my son. It was what he wanted . . . what he craved. In my pride I abandoned him for several thousand years; and then, in the last, I killed him" (Sandman 67:6). Nuala responds to this by saying, "You *want* them to punish you, don't you? You want to be punished for Orpheus's death" (67:6). Dream's wordless reply reveals the truth to her statement, in a poignant scene. At this point, Dream can no longer deny the change he has undergone, as "I told Ishtar that she was wrong. That I was not changed. That I did not change. But in truth, I think I lied to her" (67:6).

After that, there is nothing left to do. He goes off to "fight" the Kindly Ones, and ends up sitting, waiting for his older sister, Death. When she comes, he tells her, "Since I killed my son . . . the Dreaming has not been the same . . . or perhaps I was no longer the same. I still had my obligations . . . But even the freedom of the Dreaming can be a cage, of a kind, my sister" (Sandman 69:6). Dream's state can be better summarized when he tells her, "I am tired, my sister. I am very tired" (69:2). For Dream, ten billion years of life has proven to be too much. He is human now, but what he really craves is release, for perhaps there are limits on how much he can change. For now, there is nothing else to do. He takes his sister's hand, and is no more. Dream's death, then, has much more to do with his inner state than with the Furies (the ostensible cause of his death). When he takes Death's hand, he is making a choice.

Of course, to quote Bob Dylan, death is not the end, especially not for Dream. After all, how can you kill someone who is a manifestation of consciousness? When Morpheus (Dream through the first nine volumes) is destroyed, the child Daniel, who has been taken to the Dreaming, is transfigured, and becomes the new Dream. Thus, Morpheus's final act is to leave the Dreaming with a new, more human Dream. Lucien refers to this when he tells Matthew "I think he did more than *let* it happen. Charitably . . . I think . . . Sometimes, perhaps, one must change or die. And, in the end, there were, perhaps, limits to how much he could let himself change" (Sandman 71:59). Daniel, then, represents the final step in Dream's journey to become human. Daniel, in contrast to Morpheus, is aware of his emotions (as opposed to Morpheus, who was the very opposite of introspective), and not afraid to admit he is afraid, as "This is very new to me, Matthew. This place, this world. I have existed since the beginning of time. This is a true thing. I am older than worlds and suns and gods. But tomorrow I will meet my brother and sisters for the first time. And I am afraid" (Sandman 71:49). He is visibly hurt when he calls Matthew his friend, and Matthew responds "I was *his* friend. I'm not your anything" (71:49). We will see later that Matthew's inner conflict and opinion of Daniel are very important.

The confusion over identity is due in large part to the difference between the two incarnations of Dream. For example, Daniel touches the Pegasus guarding the castle door (which Morpheus never did), and it asks, "I know you are **you**, lord. But are you also *him*?" (Sandman 71:72). The confusion is perhaps alleviated when Lyta calls Dream "Daniel," and he replies, "No. What was mortal of Daniel was burned away: what was immortal was . . . transfigured. I am Dream of the Endless" (Sandman 72:87). Although Daniel's mortality was burned away, what is essential of him remains. Lyta then asks him if he (as Dream) is going to punish her. Daniel (and I refer to him as such only to avoid confusion) tells her that although he is no longer related to her, and that he may punish as he desires, that he will not punish her. Instead, he kisses her forehead, gives her protection against vengeance, and tells her to rebuild her life (72:88). Daniel's actions are in sharp contrast to Morpheus's both when he is so cold to Lyta in "The Doll's House," and when he condemns Alex Burgess (Roddy's son) to an eternal nightmare upon escaping from the glass cage. Alex's punishment, by the way, ends when Morpheus dies and Daniel takes over. In "The Wake," Daniel even shows Alex and way home. With the passing of the responsibilities to Daniel (and there being *someone* to take over the responsibilities is quite important for Dream), Morpheus's journey is complete. It might be difficult to see how a story in which the main character commits a complicated form of suicide can at the same time be seen as life-affirming, as Campbell would argue most myths are. Part of the answer lies in Campbell's first function of mythology: wonder at the majesty of life in the world. The rest lies in Daniel. Morpheus lived ten billion years, and perhaps people were not meant to live that long. Indeed, of the Endless, only Death and Destruction seem to be whole, healthy people (and Destruction is only so because he abandoned his responsibilities). But through Daniel, Dream lives on, and in a more human form than Morpheus could have provided. So even while we mourn his loss, from death comes life.

So far, we have alluded to the role of humanity in the modern myth. And we have for the most part let questions of what it means to be human go unanswered. However, at this point, we can say a few things. For there are some contradictions to address. Dream becomes human, but it quickly becomes too much for him, and he dies soon after. We have been privileging the human, but at the same time we have seen the brokenness and meaninglessness of modern life. The first paradox can be explained as a matter of time. Dream may have become human before his death, but he spent 10,000,000,000 years as not even remotely human. In a sense, part of the problem was that he was solitary for so long. In today's world, one of the essential factors of what it means to be human is relationality. Niebuhr says that "community is an individual as well as social necessity; for the individual can realize himself only in intimate and organic relation to his fellowmen [sic]" (II, 244). We exist in relationships with other people, and the rewards of these relationships are part of what makes life worth living. As we have seen, Morpheus made a mess of his relationships (ie Nada, Calliope, and Orpheus). Part of what made his existence as a human (at the end of his life) so difficult is that he had ten billion years of mistakes, ten billion years of regrets to live with. Another factor in humanity, then, is emotion. The characters that we see as most "human" are those that express deep emotion.

Desire, for example, seems to feel nothing at all, except anger towards Dream when he foils its plans. And while Dream's pre-imprisonment emotions are dramatic, they are also limited, to a kind of adolescent brooding. For Dream, becoming human was a process of feeling everything much more deeply, and of seeing the lives and emotions of others as important as well (contrast his treatment of Nuala in "The Kindly Ones" with that of Nada in condemning her to Hell).

Finally, many people in modern life are, in a sense, broken, or, as Robert Johnson says, wounded. However, another important characteristic of humans is that we heal. We have at least the potential for wholeness, in contrast to gods who remain gods, who remain limited in their expression (for Loki is always wily and destructive, and Remiel always wishy-washy). Also, compared to the gods, our lives are small. Many people lament this fact, but just because we do not literally hold up the world like Atlas, that does not mean we cannot be great. For it is the smallness of our lives (in one sense) that makes them so precious. Part of being human, then, is what Gilbert calls "the little victories, and the tiny defeats" (Sandman 16:7). Most important, humans are mortal. Because of our mortality, we feel the need to give our lives some meaning, something greater than ourselves. It is in this impulse that we create the gods, and in *Sandman*, we sustain all the different pantheons. Myths, in the end, are about *us*. And while we suffer, our suffering is balanced by joy and love. Dream had love from Nuala, and from Death, but he was still unsure enough of his newfound humanity (after all, one does not transform all at once) to gain strength from this. And though we are mortal, we are meant to be that way. Morpheus is so tired at the end because he has lived for so long. Ten billion years would be too long for anyone, if one has not been able to make peace with his or her past, as Destruction has. What we need, in the end, is rest. And for all he had changed, his glorious journey from myth to human, he was so tired that he never got to enjoy his newfound emotions. And that is his tragedy.

At this point, some of Jung's ideas can elucidate the plot of *Sandman*. First, there is the Shadow, which Jung defines as "everything that the subject refuses to acknowledge about himself and yet is always thrusting itself upon him directly or indirectly" (Archetypes 284-5). Jung also says that "everyone carries a shadow, and the less it is embodied in the individual's conscious life, the blacker and denser it is" (Psychology 93). One of the enduring mysteries of "The Kindly Ones" is just who Loki and Robin Goodfellow were working for when they kidnapped Daniel and burned his mortality away. One possibility, of course, is that Dream orchestrated the entire thing himself. And while everything ends as if he had planned the entire thing, Dream genuinely does not seem to know what is going on, especially in the early stages of the game. But it is also possible that Dream was behind the whole thing, but did not let himself know what he was doing (the left hand not knowing what the right hand is doing, if you will). And if this was the case, part of him would have to be acting secretly. Jung describes occasions when the Shadow, repository of all those parts of ourselves we choose not to recognize, breaks off from the conscious self and is forced "underground," in effect acting independently of the conscious will. This phenomenon is probably quite rare, but it would be more likely the more a person represses and forces down into his unconscious. And although Dream is a manifestation of consciousness, he is (at least at the beginning) one of the least introspective characters you will ever meet. And as a being over ten billion years old, his shadow must be a mile long (even his word-balloons are black!). This would seem to fit the mold of a being whose shadow is not incorporated into his conscious personality, so it splits off and acts on its own. Especially in "The Kindly Ones," there is so much of which Dream is unaware. Over the course of the series, Dream had already set up most of what was happening (such as by allowing Loki to remain free and in his debt), so all the "agent" would have to do was to give Loki and Robin the idea of kidnapping Daniel. So it seems possible that Dream's shadow was behind his self-destruction, and that he was a willing participant (or maybe "willing" is not a good term to use here) in his demise. Finally, while the Shadow is often dangerous, it is not necessarily evil. Jung also says that "the shadow is merely somewhat inferior, primitive, unadapted, and awkward; not wholly bad. It even contains inferior, childish, or primitive qualities which could in a way vitalize and embellish human existence . . ." (Psychology 94-5). Rather than its usual pejorative usage, "inferior" for Jung means the aspects of oneself that are not developed fully, and that one turns away from. But others might use that same function more fully. It is also interesting that Jung talks about incorporating "childish" aspects into oneself, especially in the light of Dream's transformation into Daniel, the child.

At the same time, Dream's process of becoming human and conscious of his being in many ways reflects Jung's process of "individuation," or becoming whole, in which the conscious and unconscious selves are merged. Jung says "I use the term 'individuation' to denote the process by which a person becomes a psychological 'in-dividual,' that is, a separate, indivisible unity or 'whole'" (Archetypes 275). Thus, in coming to terms with the parts of himself that cause his destruction, Dream becomes not just a whole person, but a person. For him, the individuation process is considerable indeed, spanning seventy issues. And as Jung says, "nature herself demands a death and a rebirth" (Archetypes 130). The story would not be complete without this. Leeming speaks of the death of the hero, as the hero "teaches us something of the positive nature of death as the catalyst for new birth through the spirit. As always, the hero is the symbol of man in search of himself" (181). As we will see, death, far from being something to be feared, can be seen as a positive, even blessed event.

Finally, the other place it seems appropriate to bring in Jung's terminology here is with the archetype of the child. Jung says that "the child motif is a picture of certain *forgotten* things in our childhood . . . not only something that existed in the distant past but also something that exists *now*" (Archetypes 161-2; emphasis in original). In many ways, Daniel could be seen as embodying the child archetype, as "one of the essential features of the child motif is its futurity. The child is the potential future" (Jung, Archetypes 164). Not only does Daniel represent the future, but he is at the same time small and powerful. Even as a child, he saves Matthew's life, and when questioned on his "powerlessness" as a child, he responds "And you were once a man,

Matthew. Were you entirely without power, even then? . . . Before I died, I told me many things [sic] . . ." (Sandman 71:55). Jung comments on the state of being "smaller than small yet bigger than big" (Archetypes 166). In this aspect, the child archetype resembles Daniel, who is as old as the universe, but still a child. Later, Jung says that "though the child may be 'insignificant,' unknown, 'a mere child,' he is also divine" (Archetypes 170). Daniel's transfiguration also reflects Christian themes. And part of the power of those themes comes from the fact that the child represents something in each of us. Although Daniel is special because he gestated in dreams, it is his humanity that allows him to be transformed. The final implication of Daniel's transformation is that each one of us has the immortal nature required to be transfigured into one of the Endless. Presumably, it was Daniel, but it could have been any of us, for we all have all the gods within us. And that is precisely the point of the child archetype.

Taken as a tale of transformation, *The Sandman* is what McConnell calls "a magnificent parable about the humanization of myth: about how the values of regret, responsibility, and the awful duties of love outweigh even the power and majesty of the gods we invent and then worship" ("Kindly Ones" Introduction). Remember that just like other kinds of myths, the reason we find hero sagas so compelling is not the wondrous deeds accomplished, but because the heroes, in some way, are versions of *us*. Likewise, in mythology, "not the animal world, not the plant world, not the miracle of the spheres, but man himself is now the crucial mystery" (Campbell, Hero with a Thousand Faces 391). Morpheus's journey and realization that there is something terribly wrong with his life is at once moving, strange, funny, and inspirational. And another way to look at the extent of Dream's transformation relates to his physical form. In "The Doll's House," when the Corinthian attacks Dream, the nightmare's knife goes right through Dream's hand ("Doll's House," p 173)—indeed, he scarcely notices as he uncreates his "opponent." However, in "The Kindly Ones," when one of the ladies hits Dream with a scorpion whip, he bleeds profusely (Sandman 67:19), and even retains a scar from the incident. He has become a human. In this sense, Dream's flesh and blood, real and human, are a miracle.

As a final note on Dream's death, it would be interesting to look at Dream's behavior from a perspective of mental health and depression. Dream does have a hand in his own death, after all, and his turbulent emotional life fuels the series. Terrence Real, in a book on depression in men, says this of the traditionally masculine view of showing emotion: "As a society, we have more respect for the walking wounded—those who deny their difficulties—than we have for those who 'let' their conditions 'get to them.' Traditionally, we have not liked men to be very emotional or very vulnerable. An overtly depressed man is both—someone who not only has feelings but who has allowed those feelings to swamp his competence. A man brought down by life is bad enough. But a man brought down by his own unmanageable feelings—for many, that is unseemly" (35). Clearly, Real is exhorting men to gain a greater awareness of their emotions. And I would argue that this is just what happens to Dream. He is overcome by his newfound emotions, to the point at which he can no longer function. Of course, there are larger issues at stake than in a "simple" case of mental depression; Dream, after all, has responsibilities. As we will see, Dream makes the responsible decision not to continue ignoring his emotions; rather, he arranges for a more human Daniel to take his place. And it is worth mentioning that Dream's greatest victory comes in reclaiming his emotions.

From *The Sandman*, it appears that there is still some life left in the old hero's journey. Campbell said once that the story of the hero is "what's worth writing about" (*Power of Myth*, video 1). After all, any story that involves change, and a protagonist giving up something of himself (or herself), or encountering the unknown, can be considered a hero story, perhaps all interesting tales are related to the hero myth. Perhaps what we were complaining about in the comic medium was not the inclusion of superheroes *per se*, but the banality with which they have often been rendered. That level of heightened drama, not to mention the weight of the conventions in the superhero tale, is enough to suck the life out of anything. In many ways, the Hector Hall sequence of "The Doll's House" is a parody of cheesy superhero comics. We should not be afraid, then, to call *The Sandman* a hero myth, recognizing at the same time that Dream's journey is *about* myth, which is after all what Dream is in the first place. What we have, then, is a hero myth about myth itself, as *Sandman* is a story about stories, and Dream the personification of story-telling.

That opens up the wider question of the role of heroism in *The Sandman*. We start, of course, with Dream. While most heroes have special abilities but remain fundamentally human, Dream's powers place him closer to a god (gods, of course, frequently have extraordinary powers). Part of this is intentional. Gaiman explains that at the time of the start of *Sandman* comic, publishers had redesigned Superman to give him fewer powers, under the assumption that one couldn't write interesting stories about a hero who was "too powerful." Gaiman's response was "Okay, I'll do a series that starts out with characters who are virtually all-powerful, and I'll see where I can go from there" (Bender 233-4). The danger of characters that are too powerful, it seems to me, is that they lose their sense of humanity, and are impossible to identify with. Gaiman trumped this problem by creating a character whose essential development was to become aware of the importance of humanity, and to gain access to his own. Dream's identity as a hero is further complicated by the sphere of his adventures. Most heroes leave the land of the everyday world and are initiated into magical worlds. Dream *lives* there, and in fact rules the Dreaming, one of the strangest worlds one is likely to encounter. And many of his adventures (especially "Brief Lives") take place in the waking world. Likewise, according to Campbell, an important part of the hero journey is "Atonement with the father," so perhaps it is appropriate that Dream finally comes to atonement with his son, perhaps adding to the "inverse" quality of Dream's story (in the sense of being an inverse hero myth).

Of course, Dream *does* go on some quests; "Preludes and Nocturnes" is a fairly standard quest to regain his lost tools of office. Later, he journeys back to hell in search of Nada, and finally, in "Brief Lives," he goes into the waking world (reality) with Delirium to try to find Destruction. But if facing the unknown is always a heroic act, then facing the unknown within you may be the most heroic act of all. Hence, Campbell's classic formula of "separation—initiation—return" can take place inside a hero (Hero with a Thousand Faces 30), and effect his or her personal transformation. Perhaps this is what Campbell means when he says, "Furthermore, we have not even to risk the adventure alone; for the heroes of all time have gone before us; the labyrinth is thoroughly known; we have only to follow the thread of the hero-path. And where we had thought to find an abomination, we shall find a god; where we had thought to slay another, we shall slay ourselves; where we had thought to travel outward, we shall come to the center of our own existence; where we had thought to be alone, we shall be with the world" (Hero with a Thousand Faces 25). Furthermore, tales of heroes are compelling because we are in them, as Campbell says, "The mighty hero of extraordinary powers...is each of us: not the physical self visible in the mirror, but the king within" (Hero with a Thousand Faces 365). What Gaiman has done, then, is at the same time distance himself from the conventions of comic superhero tales (no secret identity, no costume, no issue-long fight scenes), and connect his narrative with the hero-path, a kind of tale as old as mythology itself.

After that long discussion, we find ourselves back on the hero-path. And if it took us a while to accept Dream as a hero, then it should take considerably less time to recognize heroism is many of *The Sandman*'s other characters. (After all, what would be the point of including them if they did not reflect mythic themes as well?) In order to do this, though, we may have to accept a more modern, less dramatic definition of heroism, that we have seen hints of throughout this discussion. One of the consequences of living in the modern world is that there are no more dragons out there: no demons to fight, no princesses to save. But this often disheartening fact does not mean that we have to abandon the idea of heroism completely. Rather, it must be turned inward, in examination of our everyday lives. There is heroism in the kindness done to a stranger, in the friend nursed through an illness, in the embrace of a loved one. It is *this* kind of heroism that we should look for today, for it exists all around us, and this kind of heroism that can be applied to many of Gaiman's characters (of course, like any myth, *Sandman* has its fair share of the original, more dramatic, dragon-slaying type of heroism). In addition, the "new heroism" of caring for each other, which of course is hardly new, may also relate to Campbell's sociological of myth, as it essentially posits a new emphasis on relationality in how to treat each other.

One such character (and a hero of both kinds) is Rose Walker. Gaiman describes her as "sensible, kind of cool, and kind of damaged. And a heroine" (Bender 51). Rose spends much of "The Doll's House" in a quest to find her brother. She is accompanied by Gilbert, who is also Fiddler's Green, who is himself a dream become man. Gilbert's presence as a guardian is a standard mythological motif, as "the first encounter of the hero-journey is with a protective figure (often a little old crone or old man) who provides the adventure with amulets against the dragon forces he [sic] is about to pass" (Campbell, Hero with a Thousand Faces, 69). Gilbert gives Rose Morpheus' name, to call on in the case of trouble that eventually finds her. Still, "The Doll's House" is about Rose, and her heroism becomes clear when the story converges around her. When she is revealed to be the Dream Vortex, and she learns that Dream must kill her, after a little disbelief, she accepts her immanent death: "Foschrissakes! Look, just do it. Stop apologizing and just do whatever you're going to do. Okay? Just do it" (Sandman 16:11). And in fact, she would have died, if Unity (her grandmother) had not come by and relieved Rose of what made her the vortex. Second, Rose takes care of Zelda when she is dying of AIDS. She visits her every day, pays her medical bills, brings her flowers, and listens to her talk through her stutter. Although the act may not represent a great sacrifice for Rose (she tells us that she has lots of money), her kindness to someone she hardly knew before constitutes the kind of everyday heroism that can be attained in today's world. It is important to note that Rose is also wounded over the course of the stories: physically by the big-bad-wolf serial killer in "The Doll's House," and in love by young Jack in "The Kindly Ones." James Hollis mentions that "wounds quicken consciousness and, as we recall from the mythology of eternal return, are the necessary quid pro quo for enlargement" (72). She moves past her wounds, reclaims her heart, and at the end emerges as a vehicle for life.

There are also heroic attributes to many other characters. In any scheme, acceptance of one's own death is one of the key attributes of heroism. As Campbell says, "Needless to say, the hero would be no hero if death held for him any terror: the first condition is reconciliation with the grave" (Hero with a Thousand Faces 356). Robert Olson concurs, with the description of the authentic person as one who "escaped the banality of everyday existence by recognizing his finitude and courageously facing up to the fact of death" (139). Not just death: *your* death. Finally, Paul Tillich adds that "courage always includes a risk, it is always threatened by nonbeing" (155). This measure of heroism, courage in the face of death, fits not only Rose, but many of the characters in *Sandman*. Gilbert offers his life in exchange for Rose's (issue 16), and later accepts his own death at the hands of the Furies (issue 71). In "Death: The Time of Your Life," Foxglove and company go into the realm of death itself in pursuit of Hazel and little Alvie. In "The Kindly Ones," Matthew goes off with Dream to face the Furies, even though he knows that he wouldn't be coming back (only Dream's errand saves his life). Indeed, when he says to Dream, "Look. Boss. I'm not sure I'm going to get another chance to say this. Or...hell. You know what I mean. So whatever happens. It was good being your raven. Really, I mean...It was good being your friend" (*Sandman* 68:12), he is accepting not only his own death, but also affirming Dream's transformation. Matthew might not have been the first raven, but he was the first raven to be Dream's friend. Matthew, being new to the Dreaming, knows only the post-imprisonment Dream, and he in fact cares about him very much. (And as we will see later, Matthew's opinion is very important, both for mourning as a theme, and for the role of lament.) And of course, although this case is more complicated, Dream goes off to meet the Kindly Ones, knowing that he is not coming back. Thus, if the acceptance of the possibility of their own deaths is indicative of heroism, many of the characters in <u>Sandman</u> are heroic in their own way.

Returning to the theme of less dramatic, everyday-life heroism, many other characters in *Sandman* fit this description. As Campbell says, "there are small acts of heroism, too, that occur without regard to the notoriety that you attract for it" (Power 114). Campbell also cited the mother as a heroine, and in raising Alvie, not only Hazel (his biological mother), but Foxglove too is being heroic. In fact, just living with someone in a relationship can be an act of heroism, if each member is willing to give of herself. Hazel and Foxglove have their problems, but they genuinely love each other, and their relationship is one of the great and wondrous little joys of reading *Sandman*. Besides those two, the transsexual Wanda is valiant and heroic in the careful watch she keeps over Barbie, and in going outside in the hurricane to help Maisie Hill. (This also points to a new order, in which groups that have been marginalized are included.) As Campbell says, "just living with one's heart open to others in compassion is a way wide open to all" (Power 163). One way to find meaning and purpose, then, is to look through kindness to the other people in your life. Campbell loved to talk about the myth of Parsival and the Holy Grail; his interpretation of the story was that compassion is necessary to revive the Waste Land (ie Hero's Journey 196), and the same principle can be applied here. Campbell also says that "the fundamental human experience is that of compassion" (Hero's Journey 219). It is also worth mentioning that the central act in the series, Dream killing his son, is one of mercy and compassion.

In fact, this may be one of the great lessons of *Sandman*: that life is only meaningful if it is lived with someone you care about. Mikal Gilmore, in his introduction to "The Wake," says "Morpheus died for love . . . He could not understand how to care for his own heart—he could not grasp its limitations or vanities or real needs—nor could he understand or respect the true patterns in the hearts of others . . . Until, that is, the end"(11). Dream's loneliness spans volumes—just look at all the trouble he gets into because of his love-life!—and in the end, it proves to be too much. Gilmore continues, that "in the end, Morpheus's heart could not be fixed or healed . . . and

Morpheus, in these tales, has come to understand the futility of living with a heart that cannot be fixed—especially living endlessly with such a heart"(11), a wounded heart. If we are to accept the idea that we live in a desacralized world, and the religious institutions that once provided meaning are no longer working, then perhaps love is the way out. And if love can give our lives meaning, then the little acts of heroism, as well as the big-name, dragon-slaying acts of heroism, are really just things that bring us together. This sense of the importance of love and closeness fits into both the sociological and psychological functions of myth. Here, Dream could not make this happen in his own life, but he ensured the succession of someone who could. Gilmore is right in focusing on hearts. Gaiman says "Hearts are a major part of what *Sandman* is about" (Bender 61). Beneath all the art and artifice, *Sandman* has a very big, human, beating heart.

Still, Dream's great transformation is the greatest act of heroism in *The Sandman*. To effect such a change in his life after ten billion years was so revolutionary that he never would have done so, had he realized what he was doing. In the end, Dream comes to realize that it is not the gods, but the little humans who worship them, that really matter. He realizes that even myth, old as it is, is only important as it relates to us. Campbell has been criticized for focusing too much on the human condition in his discussions of myth. However, the human condition is what produces mythology, and in the end, it is what gives these stories their value. Heroes matter not because we identify with their greatness, but because they reflect our humanity. For Dream, as the personification of myth, to remain relevant, he has to become human—*become flesh*, if you will. And there is a death, even a tragic death (one could make a strong case that "The Kindly Ones" is a tragedy in classical terms), but only so there can be a rebirth. In issue 69, as Dream dies, Rose finds out that she is pregnant. And Hal points out, "There we go, then. In the midst of death, we are in life" (69:18). It was Gaiman's prodigious vision to link this with the child archetype, and to have Dream reborn as a child, but it is Dream's whole journey, in the end, that makes him truly, forever and after, a hero.

YOU CAN BE ME WHEN I'M GONE: DEATH, MORTALITY, AND CHANGE IN *THE SANDMAN*

"The idea of death, the fear of it, haunts the human animal like nothing else; it is a mainspring of human activity . . . the fear of death is indeed a universal in the human condition."

—Ernest Becker

"And sitting there, listening to her, it occurred to me that the whole of art—maybe the whole of life—is just spray-painting your name on the wall, hoping someone will see it after you've gone. And kids are to make sure that there's someone around who'll remember you when you're not around anymore."

—Foxglove

If religion is to be seen as humankind's attempt to come to terms with and make sense of the world, then certain facts cannot escape our attention. We're cold. We're scared. We hurt. And most of all: *it's going to end*. Always, staring us in the face is the fact of death, that whatever makes these bodies move is going to leave, and these vehicles, these bodies, are going to rot. It has been called the defining factor of the human condition, and something everyone must eventually face. While other species surely have some concept of death, there is no evidence that any other species ponders mortality as we do, obsessively turning it over and over in our minds, looking for a way out. In the past (and for the lucky ones, even today), the great religions served to help people come to terms with mortality, often by promising eternal life. However, today, as we have seen, the old religions do not give people comfort and shelter as they once did, and their promises of life everlasting often ring hollow. In modern times, the fields of psychotherapy and depth psychology have tried to address the fear of death. These movements peak, in some ways, with Ernest Becker's *The Denial of Death*, which posits that the fear of death is the central impetus behind human life and culture. And if myth is to fulfill its psychological function, it should find a way of addressing mortality in a way that can comfort people. And if *The Sandman* is to be a modern myth, so must it. In addition, the fact of death opens up the fact of change, as death is change of the highest magnitude. Change is a fact of life, but one many people run away from. Gaiman's *Sandman* also addresses the fact of change in our lives, especially in "Brief Lives." In that story, it becomes clear that death and change are linked.

As a body of work (or myth), *Sandman* addresses the problem of death in several ways. Most prominent, of course, is Death herself. Gaiman's choice to cast the reaper as a pretty gothette is, depending on who you ask, purely inspired or pure silliness. Beyond this, Death is kind, friendly, and wholly practical, often acting as the counterpoint to Dream's adolescent brooding. She comforts people when she comes to "take" them, and in the end, death is something that gives meaning to our lives, as every story needs an ending. In addition, we see many characters, human and god alike, dealing with mortality: either their own deaths, or in the case of Hob Gadling, with the deaths of those around them. The practice of mourning, of grieving for lost loved ones, also appears throughout *The Sandman*, most notably in "The Wake," in which the funeral for Dream is held. Finally, change is inextricably linked with death, and the principle of change is embodied in poor confused Delirium, who was once Delight. From "Brief Lives," we can see that the problem of death is contained within the problem of change. And as a whole, *Sandman* helps us make sense of death and change, and to integrate them into our lives.

The psychoanalytic view of death, in many ways, comes to fruition with Ernest Becker's *The Denial of Death*. Published as he himself was dying, Becker argues that the fear of death is the central structuring principle around which our lives are based, and that our collective institutions are meant to assuage this fear. Becker begins by saying, "the idea of death, the fear of it, haunts the human animal like nothing else; it is a mainspring of human activity—activity designed largely to avoid the fatality of death, to overcome it by denying in some way that it is the final destiny for man . . . the fear of death is indeed an universal in the human condition" (xvii). The theologian Paul Tilllich concurs, as "the anxiety of fate and death is most basic, most universal, and inescapable. All attempts to argue it away are futile" (42). Becker continues, that according to a certain school, to which he belongs, "the fear of death is natural and is present in everyone, that it is the basic fear that influences all others, a fear from which no one is immune, no matter how disguised it may be" (Becker 15). Campbell concurs with this idea, saying that "the secret cause of all suffering is mortality itself, which is the prime condition of life. It cannot be denied if life is to be affirmed" (Power xiii). Becker also claims that the fear of death is so powerful as to be repressed, and that people come to believe that death will not happen to *them*, as "the narcissism is what keeps men marching into point-blank fire in wars: at heart one doesn't feel *he* will die, he only feels sorry for the man next to him" (2).

Another result of this fear is the creation of the hero system, by which people feel they can attain some sort of immortality, and "the hope and belief is that the things that man creates in society are of lasting worth and meaning, that they outlive or outshine death and decay, that man and his products count" (5). We also come to see the hero as someone who bravely faces death: "when we see a man bravely facing his own extinction we rehearse the greatest victory we can imagine" (Becker 12). We have already seen from Campbell the acceptance of death as an important facet of heroism; Becker makes it the central, even defining feature. And as a result of bravely accepting his or her own death, the hero attains some kind of immortality. At least, that is how things once worked. Today, Becker says, religion and culture no longer serve to help mediate the fear of death; "religion is no longer valid as a hero system, and so the youth scorn it" (7). The question that remains from Becker is how to regain that sense of comfort, the valid hero system. The answer put forth, here at least, is the modern myth.

Many of Becker's formulations are reflected in parts of *The Sandman*. At one point, Foxglove, while attending a funeral, says, "And sitting there, listening to her, it occurred to me that the whole of art—maybe the whole of life—is just spray-painting your name on the wall, hoping someone will see it after you've gone. And kids are to make sure that there's someone around who'll remember you when you're not around anymore" (Time of Your Life 83). Here again we see death as a defining feature in life, and art and culture and religion and anything else you can think of as an attempt to deal with this overwhelming fact. To continue this point, an angel in Gaiman's short story "Murder Mysteries" describes the process by which the angels work out details of the universe before the creation. Here, it describes the "process" for death: "And our latest project was *Death*. It's one of the hard ones—one of the big ones, too, I suspect. Possibly it may even become the attribute that's going to define the Creation for the Created: If not for *Death*, they'd be content to simply exist, but with *Death*, well, their lives will have meaning—a boundary beyond which the living cannot cross" (Gaiman, Angels & Visitations 151-2). Thus, while death is central, it also provides meaning to life. To be complete, every story must have an ending, and death is ours. (Bettie, the waitress in "24 Hours," says that all stories end in death if you stay with them long enough. This idea, of our lives as a narrative, will be discussed in later sections.)

A large part of Becker's argument is devoted to people's realization of their dual nature: we are conscious beings, able to ponder the mysteries of the universe, but we are also enfleshed, in temples of meat, bodies we know will eventually cease to support us, as "this is the paradox: he is out of nature and hopelessly in it; he is dual, up in the stars and yet housed in a heart-pumping, breath-gasping body that once belonged to a fish and still carries the gill-marks to prove it" (Becker 26). Many people reject their bodies, identifying only with their consciousness. But doing this cuts one off from an important part of oneself. Gaiman (through Eve) tells a story about bodies, and the wives of Adam. After Lilith went away, God created a second wife for Adam, from the inside out, while he watched. And when he saw her, he was disgusted and rejected her; the story serves as a prelude to the creation of Eve. Eve, telling the story, says, "Adam couldn't bear to go near her. He wouldn't touch her. 'He saw her full of secretions and blood.' That's what the Midrash states. Bodies are strange.

Some people have real problems with the stuff that goes on inside them. You find out that inside someone you know there's just mucus and meat and slime and bone. They menstruate, salivate, defecate and cry" (Sandman 40:15). The point of the story, it seems to me, is to accept the "creatureliness" both in yourself and in people around you. If we are of a dual nature, then we can never be whole if we deny half of it. In *Sandman*, as in life, bodies are important.

Gaiman, on many occasions in *Sandman*, devotes a great deal of space to the problem of death. The most important "defense" provided against the anxiety of death comes in the form of the character of Death. First, there are her general mannerisms. Paying attention to cultural mores, after Bergman as much as anyone else, one would expect Death to be cold, dark, and brooding. I suspect that Gaiman had this in mind when he created his Death. To put it bluntly, Death is too cute for words. When she first sees Dream (the first time we see her), she jokes and quotes Mary Poppins (Sandman 8:5). If Death is supposed to be foreboding, someone forgot to tell her. When Destiny calls a family meeting, Death shows up in jeans and a tank top. When Destiny suggests more formal attire, she says, "Aw, c'mon. You know how much I hate wearing that stuff . . . Next thing you're going to be moaning that I ought to get a scythe" (Sandman 21:5), but she relents to make her brother happy. When Orpheus comes to her house, he finds a "homey" place, with teddy bears, goldfish, and black stockings lying around (Orpheus 21). Hardly what one would expect from the "lord of death." Later, she acts as the practical counterpoint to Dream's brooding. When she finds Dream moping, she yells at him, "You are utterly the stupidest, most self-centered, appallingest excuse for an anthropomorphic personification on this or any other plane! An infantile, adolescent, pathetic specimen! Feeling all sorry for yourself because your little game is over, and you haven't got the—the balls to go and find a new one! I don't believe this. Dream, you're as bad as—as Desire! Or worse!" (Sandman 8:9-10). Here, she gives Dream exactly what he needs—some straight talk.

Still, she is not always harsh. She invites Dream to come with her, and on the ensuing journey, he finds peace and meaning; this is the plot of issue 8, "The Sound of Her Wings." Later, at the family meeting, Death sides with Desire, telling Dream that condemning Nada to Hell for rejecting his love was "a really shitty thing to do" (Sandman 21:22). Still, she does not needle Dream, as Desire does; she simply tells him that he was wrong, and that he had better make it right. In the end, Death is purely pragmatic and realistic, yet often lighthearted and silly. Gaiman mentions that "if you look at the numerous anthropomorphic representations of Death over the years, you'll find that most of them are scary, humorless, implacable people who you really wouldn't want to spend time with" (Bender 238). The impetus behind Gaiman's Death, then, would seem to be someone you would actually look forward to meeting. Campbell speaks of a Muslim belief about the Angel of Death, that "when the Angel of Death approaches, he is terrible. When he reaches you, it is bliss" (Power 222). Of course, they got the pronoun wrong, but they had the right idea. In *Sandman*, Death is humanized, helping to defray some of the fear of death.

A second way the character of Death answers the fear of death is in the way she acts toward those she has come to "take." In physical terms, she always reaches a hand out to the person, to the old man in issue 8, to Hob Gadling in "The Wake" (although he does not die), and, most significantly, to Dream at the end of "The Kindly Ones." When the dying ask her what happens next, she always says, "Now's when you find out." If Neil knows what happens after death, he isn't telling. But there is a certain "rightness" to not finding out what happens until you actually die. To know beforehand would take away all the mystery and meaning. And as Gaiman often says, it is the mystery that remains, and matters. And although her job may be a hard one, she performs it with care. When Bernie Capax, aged 15,000 years, is killed by a falling wall, he asks Death, "But I did okay, didn't I?" She answers as she reaches out to him: "You lived what anybody gets, Bernie. You got a lifetime. No more. No less. You got a lifetime" (Sandman 43:5). After she takes the old man, she says to Dream, "I thought he was sweet. Didn't you?" (Sandman 8:15).

Later in that issue, she says "gets me down, too. Mostly they aren't too keen to see me. They fear the sunless lands." (8:17). Dream fills in the discussion by telling us, "I find myself wondering about humanity. Their attitude to my sister's gift is so strange. Why do they fear the sunless lands? It is as natural to die as it is to be born. But they fear her. Dread her. Feebly attempt to placate her. They do not love her" (8:19). He then recalls a poem celebrating death that, according to the Sandman Annotations (http://rtt.colorado.edu/~jnmiller/Sandman.html), comes from Campbell's *Masks of God* series. The poem begins, "Death is before me today: / Like the recovery of a sick man, / Like going forth into a garden after sickness" (8:19-20). Moreover, as the whole issue gives us a glimpse of Death performing her duties, the poem is interlaced (in an effect that could only be gained in a visual medium like comics) with images of people dying. In the end, Dream leaves her, as "I walk by her side, and the darkness lifts from my soul. I walk with her, and I hear the gentle beating of mighty wings . . ." (Sandman 8:20). The phrase "the gentle beating of mighty wings" is a refrain throughout the issue, and underscores Death's gentleness, even as she performs the most feared of functions. In the end, we see Death as someone not to be feared, but revered as the mediator between this life and whatever lies beyond it. The point here is that death is part of the natural process, and far from being someone we should fear, it (she) can be seen as a blessed function, and a friendly face.

One of the purest examples of Death performing and describing her duties comes in her meeting with Raine Blackwell (a little-known comic character, called "Element Girl," who can transmute herself into any element) in "Facade" (issue 20). Death has actually come for someone down the hall, but she hears Raine crying. Raine desperately wants to die, but can't figure out a way to do so. And although she does not "take" Raine, Death tells her how to find the god (Ra) who made her the way she is, and indirectly, how to end her life. But Death's helping Raine is not highlighted so much as Death's speech beforehand. She says: "Anyway: I'm not blessed, or merciful. I'm just me. I've got a job to do, and I do it. Listen: Even as we're talking, I'm there for old and young, innocent and guilty, those who die together and those who die alone. I'm in cars and boats and planes, in hospitals and forests and abattoirs. For some folks death is a release, and for others death is an abomination, a terrible thing. But in the end, I'm there for all of them. Raine, in West Africa a small village is being massacred by mercenaries, in pay of their own government. I'm there. In the farthest reaches of a distant galaxy, a planet is being ripped apart by internal stresses; the planet was the home of many crystal intelligences, calm and fine and beautiful. I am there as well" (Sandman 20:20). While death does not consider herself good or bad, the way she outlines her responsibilities is in fact comforting and assuages our deepest fears. For not only is Death the end of our lives, she is one of the Endless, the structuring principles of the universe, and she is said to be the only one of the Endless to survive past this form of the universe (more of Campbell's cosmological function). She finishes her speech, that "When the first living thing existed, I was there, waiting. When the last living thing dies, my job will be finished. I'll put the chairs on the tables, turn out the lights and lock the universe behind me when I leave" (20:20). There is something both profound and poetic about that speech. Indeed, Death is sometimes blessed, in the case of Raine, or even with Dream. One of the lessons of "The Kindly Ones" is that even for gods, or the Endless, who are more than gods, eternity may be too much. We simply are not meant to live forever.

As side-stories, the two Death miniseries, "The High Cost of Living" (HCL) and "The Time of Your Life" (TYL) showcase Death's more human side. (She is already quite human compared to, say, Dream, but here we see her outside the context of her responsibilities.) In the first, we see Death on her once-a-century day as a mortal. As background, once a century, Death becomes human and mortal for one day, so as to understand the bitter tang of mortality, and to understand the life for which she serves as a boundary. As she goes through her day, she often expresses wonder and amusement at the world; for example "is the chemical aftertaste the reason why people eat hot dogs? Or is it some kind of bonus?" (HCL II:4). This wonder and amusement fit easily into what Campbell termed the mystical first function of myth. Speaking to the universality of Death, she says "I know everybody really well" (II:11). By all accounts, Death is a very good human, and in a conversation with herself, she says that she greatly enjoyed the experience, and wishes it could have gone on longer. As human Death says, "I wish it could have gone on forever. I wish it didn't have to end like that." (HCL III:19) The Endless Death replies, "it always ends. That's what gives it value"Thus, we see that the desire for life is quite universal. In the second series, she allows baby Alvin to live, "because, once, I got to touch life without taking it. Nostalgia, sentiment, fondness . . ." (TYL 76). Finally, in the second series, Death reaffirms the universal human dignity, what the Quakers call the "divine spark." She says, "Nobody's creepy from the inside, Hazel. Some of them are sad, and some of them hurt, and some of them think they're the only real thing in the whole world. But they're not creepy" (TYL 42). Death, then, is someone who sees the good in everyone.

Death's final moment of centrality in *Sandman* comes at Dream's funeral. For the occasion, she is dressed entirely in red, instead of her usual black, and she makes the final speech of the funeral, as "now the girl in the red dress talks to you all, as the boat begins its passage down the slow stream. And her words make sense of everything. She gives you peace. She gives you meaning. And she bids her brother goodbye" (Sandman 72:82). Death's appearance at Dream's funeral also opens up the larger issue of mourning. Not all of our death-anxiety is focused on the idea of our own deaths. Some of it concerns the pain and emptiness of saying goodbye to people we have loved. So after 69 issues of getting to know Dream, watching him become human, and seeing him die, another "test" of Gaiman's creation is whether or not the final volume of the series, called "The Wake," can comfort us. The centerpiece of the funeral is the speeches given by the other members of the Endless, and by Dream's friends. Despair says, "This is the second brother I have lost . . . And it hurts. I cared for him, very much. He was so wise; he seemed so certain of the rightness of his actions. And I, who do nothing but doubt, admired that in him. He was a creature of hope. For dreams are hopes, and echoes of hopes. And I am a creature of despair" (Sandman 72:76). Despair, at this moment, is all the hurt and fear and loss that we feel, a counterpoint to the hope provided by Dream as well as others. Her speech is also another clue that the series is about hope. And while Despair's speech makes us feel heavily the loss of one we loved, later speeches bring hope and comfort. Perhaps the strongest example of this comes from the angel Duma, still silent even though he has been exiled from the Silver City to rule Hell. Duma says nothing, and lets fall a single tear: "And the Angel Duma's tear, crystalline and clear, filled the vision of each of the onlookers. Reflected in it, they saw mercy and miracles, and the knowledge that every thing that is, has a purpose, and that the purpose, somehow, included every one of them . . . on a deep and personal level" (72:77). During moments of death, we want nothing more than to be enveloped in a plan of some god's (or God's) love, to know that we are included, that our lives mean something, and that we are loved. Earlier in the series, the angel Remiel's "best of all possible worlds" speech is shown to be an echo of an empty morality and inappropriate optimism (after all, he *is* in Hell . . .). But Duma's "speech," in one fleeting moment, succeeds where Remiel's did not. The point of this is for the mourner (or reader) to walk away feeling somehow *absolved* (in the sense of grief and guilt being removed).

Although Death and Duma may have the most powerful speeches, in many ways, the heart of "The Wake" is Matthew the raven. At the beginning, Matthew feels guilt for leaving Dream (albeit at Dream's request) and wants nothing more than to die, as "I could have died. I could have died when the others died. I could have died at his side . . . If I'd died then I wouldn't be here being miserable now" (Sandman 70:28). He is unfriendly towards Daniel, and perhaps this is understandable. He misses the Dream he knew. Gaiman explains that "Matthew played a very important role in 'The Wake.' Daniel is actually much gentler and kinder than the Sandman we've followed throughout the series, but the fact remains that he's not *our* Sandman. So we're simply not going to like Daniel right away. Matthew therefore gets to be us. I wanted him to stand for every reader who was pissed off about the Sandman being dead, who missed the old Dream and felt he was irreplaceable" (Bender 216). Thus, Matthew feels the sorrow and guilt (because he "abandoned" Dream, and because he is gone) we all feel. So much, in fact, that he wants Daniel to let him die, as he has no interest in being Daniel's raven. However, after thinking about it, he begins to change his mind. This process begins with his speech at the funeral. "I was going to say something about how he died. And about how that's what I wanted to do. But that isn't what's in my heart. Not really. He was the most important person in the world to me, and he's gone. And the kid, Daniel . . . Well, he was a good kid, and he's gone too. [That is, he is no longer "Daniel".] But you can't kill dreams, not really. *I mean, despair may be the thing that comes after hope, but there's still hope, right? When there's no hope you might as well be dead.* What's in my heart? A lot of sorrow. A little regret. And the memory of the coolest, strangest, most infuriating boss . . . friend . . . boss . . . I ever had" (Sandman 72:80, emphasis mine). This might be Dream's most fitting epitaph. Still, it is important to note Matthew's invocation of hope. One of the central ideas in *The Sandman* is that hope will always survive. Matthew's change comes to be an affirmation of life. When Daniel asks if he still wants to "move on" (die), Matthew says "I had to make a speech about the boss at the shindig . . . and while I was talking, I think I figured a few things out for myself . . . *Funeral's over. Time to get on with our lives. Time to grow up*" (Sandman 72:89, emphasis mine). Commenting on this speech, Hy Bender says "ultimately, growing up is what *Sandman* is about" (207). Mourning has its place, and while it should never be trivialized, there comes a time to move on. This is the sentiment that guides "The Wake," as we say goodbye to Dream. This theme is also visible in Rose Walker's decision to leave her room at the end of "Doll's House" (more on this incident later).

Another place in *Sandman* of mourning, actually an echo of Dream's funeral, comes at the end of the reality storm in "World's End." Brant, watching the funeral procession, talks about his father's funeral, and how he found it empty, as "So I put on a suit and went to the funeral, and came away . . . disappointed. The whole routine seemed as foolish and empty as the plastic flowers in the 'Chapel of Rest,' a meaningless act, a shadow of something real. The words said over my father's body were hollow and dumb, and I couldn't find it in me to cry, not then" (Sandman 56:15). In contrast, he is deeply affected by Dream's procession, as "I knew I was watching the real thing here. There was true grief in each step they took across the sky, and they shouldered the casket as if they were shouldering the weight of the world. And they walked. I could feel something hot and burning on my cheeks, and my eyes began to sting. I don't know who I was crying for, and I hated myself for it; but I couldn't look away" (56:15). Now he is truly able to mourn. Then he sees Death at the end of the procession; "I think I fell in love with her, a little bit. Isn't that dumb? But it was like I knew her. Like she was my oldest, dearest friend. The kind of person you can tell anything to, and they'll still love you, because they know you . . . I'll always love her. All my life" (56:18-19). The image of Death, in grief, looking at him, is so poignant and compelling that no description can do it justice. And of course Brant's description of Death is an apt one. Earlier in "World's End," we encounter Destruction talking to one of the keepers of the Necropolis, the city of funeral rites. He says that "it's important to have places like this. Once the spirit's flown and the spark of life has gone, then rituals of farewell are needed. All the rituals we go through to help us say goodbye. You *have* to say goodbye" (55:15). Finally, during the funeral procession in "World's End," Brant at one point says "There they were. In the sky. And I believed in miracles. I didn't have any choice" (Sandman 56:17). Campbell's first function of myth is a kind of mystical wonder. Here, in a moment of death, we have one of the strongest affirmations of this function. One of the lessons of *The Sandman* is to always believe in miracles.

Finally, there are small touches, little pieces tucked away in other stories, that tell us about mortality. In "The Kindly Ones," there are two short poems. As Dream returns to the Dreaming to face the Furies, the first reads: "All around me darkness gathers, / Fading is the sun that shone. / We must speak of other matters: / You can be me when I'm gone" (Sandman 67:16). This poem focuses on the coming death of Dream, and it flows well into the second, which appears at the very end of the volume as a fortune-cookie fortune: "Flowers gathered in the morning, / Afternoon they blossom on, / Still are withered by the evening: / You can be me when I'm gone" (69:24). The second poem encompasses the whole sweep of life, from youth to middle age to old age to death, with the metaphor of cut flowers. It also repeats the ending line "You can be me when I'm gone." This relates most directly to Daniel, who takes over as the new Dream, but could also be read as saying that we never completely go away, as some trace of us is left after we are gone.

Finally, there is Hob Gadling. As a *de facto* immortal, for whom death will come only when he desires it, he has plenty of time to learn about life and death. In "The Kindly Ones," we see him at the grave of woman he loved, as "Everyone's died. Everyone I've loved. My wives. My loves. My children. You know, there's something it took me a couple of centuries to figure out. I mean, there was a while when I thought that life was all about fighting and eating and sex . . . But one day I realized that it was sort of empty if you weren't with someone you wanted to spend time with" (Sandman 59:7). In "The Wake," we see Hob (with another girlfriend), and his encounter with Death, who wants to see if he is ready to die yet. Hob goes on about death taking away things and people until "one day you walk round your house and there's nothing there to keep you, nothing to make you want to stay . . . Lots of little deaths until the big one" (Sandman 73:111). In the end, he says no to Death's offer. In effect, he is saying that even though we miss the ones we love, we can always meet more people with whom to fill our lives, and that we need not ever feel alone. This philosophy might seem immature (as Hob often does), but there is some truth to it. In addition, it amounts to what Campbell calls "an affirmation of life," and elsewhere "the act of joyful participation in the sorrows of the world" (Hero's Journey 226). We should never reach the point where we are no longer interested in new experiences. If we do, then we're already dead.

So far, we have focused on the role of death (and Death) in *The Sandman*. However, in "Brief Lives" death is revealed to be a part of a larger whole, of change. It is useful, then, to examine the role of change in that volume. And no one embodies change quite like Delirium, who drives the action of the story. She continually talks in non-sequiturs, and flits about, changing her appearance by the moment (she never does look the same way twice). Even her word-balloons are multicolored, and strangely shaped. Her eyes are mismatched, one green and one blue. It is she that initiates the search for Destruction, because she misses him, and wants their family to be whole again. Thus, she resists change, even changes that happened 300 years ago. Indeed, she knows change better than anyone. For Delirium was once Delight. At one point, she remembers "the moment she realized what was happening, that the universe was changing, that she was growing up or at least growing older . . . She was no longer Delight; and the blossoms had already begun to fall in her domain, becoming smudged and formless colors, and she had no one to talk to . . . Then [Destruction] said, 'Del. Things are changing.' She knew it was true. And there was nothing she could do about it" (Sandman 42:20). And there are hints that even that change was not the end, as Destruction later tells Delirium, "I trust that when your next change comes, it proves easy on you," to which she responds, "change?" (Sandman 49:17).

We never find out what caused Delirium's change; if Neil knows, then he isn't telling. Thus, Delirium is in a permanent state of flux. Later, she says that she likes being on airplanes, because "I like anywhere that isn't a proper place. I like in-betweens" (Sandman 48:4). And it is a *very bad* idea to let her drive. Early in "Brief Lives," she asks Dream about several words. The last time, she asks "um. What's the name of the word for things not being the same always. You know, I'm sure there is one. Isn't there? There must be a word for it . . . the thing that lets you know time is happening. If there a word?" Dream answers her, "Change," to which Delirium responds, "oh. I was afraid of that" (Sandman 43:24). Here, as she sometimes does, Delirium says more than she means, about being afraid of change. As Peter Straub points out, fear of change is what drives the volume (5).

The theme of change also occurs with other characters in

"Brief Lives." Of course, there is Destruction, who abandoned his realm 300 years ago, the event that begins all the action of the story. Before that fateful day, he gives some notice of what is going on in his mind, as he says, to Dream, "times are changing, my brother" (Sandman 44:18). He reacts to the coming of the Enlightenment, an age of reason, which will culminate in "the flames . . . the big bang. The loud explosions" (44:21). He is growing weary of his role, and he asks "and for how much longer?" will there continue the cycle of creation and destruction? He says that the coming of reason will end in annihilation, as "then follows my time, brother. The age of fire and flame" (44:22). Besides Destruction, of course, there is Dream, who does not realize how much he has changed. Destruction says to him, "I suppose I had vaguely hoped that you had changed, my brother. That you'd noticed that there were other people in the world. That you had begun to see people as other than things that dream, as creatures of stories" (Sandman 48:8). Of course, Dream has done these things, and his actions towards his son at the end of "Brief Lives" show us how much he has changed.

Then there is radical change. The end of worlds, of gods, of ideas. Destruction is in touch with this kind of change, as he bids Dream and Delirium to come outside: as "I like the stars. It's the illusion of permanence, I think. I mean, they're always flaring up and caving in and going out. But from here, I can pretend . . . I can pretend that things last. I can pretend that lives last longer than moments. Gods come, and gods go. Mortals flicker and flash and fade. Worlds don't last; and stars and galaxies are transient, fleeting things that twinkle like fireflies and vanish into cold and dust. But I can pretend" (Sandman 48:12-13). Nothing in the universe is permanent, no matter what the time scale is, and pretending is one of the things that make it all okay. Destruction continues this line of thought, as: "The Endless? The Endless are merely patterns. The Endless are ideas. The Endless are wave functions. The Endless are repeating motifs. The Endless are echoes of darkness, and nothing more. We have no right to play with their lives, to order their dreams and desires. And even our existences are brief and bounded. None of us will last longer than this version of the universe [except Death]" (48:16). Even the Endless have finite lives, and they will in time cease to exist. As Straub says, "What is of brief duration (*and any duration is brief*) is to be embraced, valued, reluctantly surrendered" (emphasis mine). The Endless are not exempt from change, the last of which is death. (It is worthwhile to note that in the series, the only members of the Endless who resemble fully functioning human beings are Death and Destruction.) And as we have seen, the heroic thing to do in the face of mortality is to accept it, even embrace it. And the lesson here is that even the Endless, who are supposed to be eternal, are subject to change, as are all beings. There is an irony here. The Endless are subject to change, and are not as eternal as we thought. Humans become immortal, while gods are mortal. Essentially, we have a blurring of the boundaries between human, god, and Endless; the unifying factor is change.

Finally, there is Peter Straub's afterword, "On Mortality and Change," which merits some attention in itself. He says, "The concept of change, of drastic change to come and unalterable changes that have already occurred, haunts 'Brief Lives'" (2). He says that even eternity can be brief, and that we all resist change. Later, he mentions that "Destruction points out that his brother's morality has evolved, and Dream coldly denies this suggestion. It would amount to an acknowledgement of change, and he resists change" (4) Of course, Dream reaches the point at which even he has to admit he has changed. Straub also says that "Wisdom is a matter of recognizing that nothing stands still, that everything is hurtling toward its own conclusion. Wisdom is in the celebration and memorialization of the temporal" (2). We fear change because it means mortality. But the fact of change, or death, is simply what gives our lives, our stories, as Gaiman is fond of saying, meaning. Thus, death is part of change, and all change is the death of something, be it a person, an idea, or a way of life.

In the end, we are left, once more, with the human condition. We know that one day we are going to die. Becker claims that the fear of death is so terrifying that we repress it, only to have it surface indirectly in everything we do. However, this fear is not always unconscious; rather, it is a thought's breath away, as we are never far from thinking about death. If a person were to try to create a myth, a modern myth, he or she would have to account for the cold, hard fact of mortality. It is possible to see Gaiman's formulation of Death as someone you would actually want to spend time with as wish fulfillment, but that would be missing the point. The purpose of a myth (or one of them, anyway) is to move people through the stages of their lives, all the meaningful rites of passage. This is what Campbell called the fourth function of myth: the psychological; and *The Sandman* does help us through our lives by living the story; as we will see, it is possible to take on a story of one's own, and by it to guide one's life. Here, Death (and death) give our lives meaning, as every story needs an ending. And she even becomes human once in a while, so as to better understand what it's like.

In addition to the character Death, a significant amount of attention is paid to the process of mourning. We mourn Dream, as we mourn for any loved one, and this process cannot be circumvented. And here, *Sandman* is like a concerned hug from a friend, saying "it's going to be okay." And it is. Because after death, there is always hope. And hope again is another one of the things that *Sandman* is about. Thus, even the knowledge that eventually, everything we see will pass away (people, gods, the stars, even the universe), that there will always be hope. The effect, then, is an affirmation of life, in all its frailties, with all its pain and sorrows, and even with its brief duration, remembering that all lives are brief.

It is no surprise that, among readers, the favorite characters are Death (mortality) and Delirium (change). Both serve as a counterpoint to Dream's brooding, Death with her common sense and straight talk, and Delirium with her delightful nonsequiturs, which every once in a while let slip a profound truth. Although the story is Dream's (and this should not be forgotten), Death and Delirium both have important lessons to teach us, about what Campbell called "how to live a human lifetime." And that, in a sense, is what any myth is about.

ISSUES OF FREEDOM, RESPONSIBILITY, AND THE PROBLEM OF EVIL IN *THE SANDMAN*

"The arbitrary and indiscriminate way in which suffering is apportioned whether by violence or by the ultimate part of suffering that cannot be ascribed to human violence . . . keeps rekindling the old questions: not just Why? But Why me? Why my beloved child."

—Paul Ricoeur

"A king will forsake his kingdom. Life and death will clash and fray. The oldest battle begins once more."

—The Grey Sisters, also called the Fates

In the study of religion, issues of freedom and responsibility have often been central. For hundreds of years, scholars and theologians have endeavored to determine to what extent we are responsible for our actions. The largest question in this debate centers around our freedom to act; simply put: are we free to act as we choose? Some have held that our actions are decided, even manipulated, beforehand, and that we thus do not enjoy true freedom, even if we feel like we do. According to this view, the world works according to a fixed set of laws, so that it would be theoretically possible to predict everything that would happen. This issue has important implications, because if we cannot determine our destiny, then logically, we should not be responsible for the actions we commit. If freedom is one side of the coin, responsibility is the other, and the question of who is responsible for any action is an important theological issue. In another sense, in this life we surround ourselves with people, and the relationships that we form are one way of defining who we are. Indeed, our relationships with others are an important part of what it means to be human. Any myth, then, should address issues of freedom and responsibility: how free we are to choose our destiny, and the responsibilities we bear towards other people. The issue of freedom and responsibility has other implications as well. In particular, if we are free to act, then we will face the possibility of performing evil acts, of destroying as well as creating. The problem of evil is one that has puzzled theologians since St. Augustine. Why does evil exist? If God is benevolent and omnipotent, why does He (or She) allow evil to happen? Why do we suffer? If one were crafting a modern myth, it should reflect the problem of evil, in a way that is relevant to people today.

In *The Sandman*, Neil Gaiman addresses issues of freedom and responsibility at several points. In the world he has created, events are in a sense foretold; Destiny, the oldest of the Endless, carries and is chained to a great book that contains all of our destinies. The three Fates of Greek myth are frequently present (as but one of the forms of the Triple Goddess), especially in "The Kindly Ones," in which the title characters measure out the thread of the story, and of Dream's life. However, even if events have been foretold, we are still responsible agents, and we must live with the consequences of what we do. Despite Destiny's book, we *feel* free to act, and our reasons for doing so are our own. For this reason, we will not concern ourselves too much with the question of free will; rather, we will assume that we are free to act, even if those actions are multiply determined.

And as we form relationships, we become responsible for others as well. *Sandman* is filled with stories of rulers forsaking their kingdoms: Destruction of his realm, Lucifer of Hell, Gilbert / Fiddler's Green of his place in the Dreaming, and (in a sense) Dream. In each of these cases, the agent's responsibilities become too much for him, and for his own health or satisfaction, he must leave his realm. Dream, in particular, is very conscious of his responsibilities as one of the Endless, and of following the rules that bind Endless and gods alike. However, in the end, even following those rules is revealed to be a kind of choice, and Dream is forced to attend to his own well-being. The lesson here is that, difficult as it may be, one can always walk away, just as Lucifer and Destruction do. Finally, the idea of responsibility is pushed even further when we learn that, Heaven or Hell, we are each responsible for our own souls, and where they end up.

Furthermore, if people are free to choose their own actions, it seems clear that some of them will choose evil. Evil, then, exists both as wrongs committed, and as suffering undergone. Here, Paul Ricoeur's categories of blame and lament are useful. As we have seen, one of the functions of myth is to explain evil, and to give people a conceptual framework with which to understand evil. In previous theologies, people have sought to find some kind of meaning or system behind the suffering of the world: people suffer because of this, or the suffering has that meaning. However, we have just concluded the bloodiest century in human history: one in which factories were made for the sake of killing, and ovens for burning the dead. In the face of such horrors, it seems that we cannot find meaning or logic to what has happened. Rather, we are forced to acknowledge it and move on. As a modern myth, *Sandman* does not try to explain why we suffer; we are simply left with the fact that we do. And just as one function of myth is to tell people of the dangers of the world (as it once did with the unknown or certain places where monsters were said to live), of demons, devils, and things that go bump in the night, here Gaiman provides us with the example of the modern demon: the serial killer. In doing so, he confronts the romanticization of such violence, and tries to understand how the minds of killers work. With other characters in the story, it is difficult, if not impossible, to find characters who are purely evil. The idea of pure evil is one that no longer functions: we see that there is no evil, only people trying to meet their own needs, and suffering undergone. No one hurts just to hurt, with the possible exception of the Corinthian. Rather, we are confronted with the fact that the face of evil is a human face: our own.

On the topic of humans' destiny and nature, Reinhold Niebuhr discusses themes of freedom and responsibility, and can furnish us with a starting point. According to him, people are free to act. He lays out self-determination as humans' essence, as "the essence of man is his freedom" (Niebuhr I, 16, 17). Niebuhr adds that "[humans have] a freedom of spirit that transcends both nature and reason" (I, 96). Each human being is a free individual, able to act as he or she chooses: "freedom of the spirit is the cause of real individuality" (Niebuhr I, 55). And if each person is an individual, it is his or her duty to act according to his or her nature, as "the source of the soul's duty lies in the soul's own nature" (Niebuhr, I 63). It is humans' freedom that makes them truly special, and different from the determining forces of nature. As Niebuhr says, "Human personality has a depth and uniqueness which escapes the ordinary processes of knowledge" (I, 294). In Niebuhr, we find a respect for the magnitude and grandeur of people's freedom. Each of us is a free agent. This theme of freedom is carried out in *Sandman*, as we are free to act as we choose in any situation. Of course, there is another side to this, and that is responsibility. Just as we are radically free, we are also radically responsible for the choices we make. In the end, we are responsible to those we love, but above all, to ourselves.

Another quotation of Niebuhr's seems to fit the contradictions of Dream: "man is both strong and weak, both free and bound, both blind and far-seeing. He stands at the juncture of spirit; and is involved in both freedom and necessity" (I, 181). Dream is supremely powerful, yet he is unable to master his own emotions. He is free to act, yet sees himself (until the end) as constrained. He possesses great foresight in selecting Daniel to succeed him, but he is unable to see what is going on within himself. All of these paradoxes come to fit Dream, as a being in transition, summed up in the phrase "man is most free in the discovery that he is not free" (Niebuhr I, 260).

The theme of freedom and responsibility comes to the fore in *Sandman*, in which Dream repeatedly refers to his responsibilities as one of the Endless. In a text description of the Endless, Gaiman says "of all the Endless, save perhaps Destiny, [Dream] is most conscious of his responsibilities, the most meticulous in their execution" (Sandman 21:11). After he escapes from his imprisonment, he sets out to rebuild his realm, and spends much time and energy in performing his responsibilities. He engages in these tasks throughout the series, although he does have time for personal tasks (like the search for his missing brother). In the short story issues, we often encounter Dream in the context of his position as one of the Endless. However, the transformation that overtakes him, that is the plot of the series writ large, soon comes to interfere with his work. The first hint we see of this takes place at the end of "Brief Lives." When he returns from his search, he tells Lucien, "Tomorrow, I shall return to my duties. I have neglected them long enough. And I have responsibilities here, after all. I have many responsibilities . . . I am certain that there is much else that needs my attention. But not today. These things can wait. Tomorrow, I shall work. But not today . . ." (Sandman 49:15-6). He then goes inside to wash Orpheus's blood off his hands. At this point, his grief and remorse are too great for him to resume his duties as one of the Endless. And rather than see this as a shirking of responsibility, it is a sign of Dream's journey towards becoming human. We get the impression that in ancient times, Dream performed his duties without any real emotional experience; after all, it was part of his nature as one of the Endless. Of course, the exception to this is in the case of his failed love affairs, which interfere significantly with the Dreaming, but he always returns to his work. In the case of Orpheus, his past mistakes have caught up with him, and he mourns for the loss of his son. The image at the end of "Brief Lives" of Dream overcome by grief for his son is one of the most poignant moments in the series.

Dream's changing relationship with responsibility and his past is also featured at the end of "A Season of Mists." In an incident already recounted here, Dream at last talks with Nada, the lover he imprisoned 10,000 years ago. He realizes that he hurt Nada grievously, and that there is nothing he can do, no apology he can give, to make that right. What else deserves to be mentioned is that after he offers Nada (again) a position as his queen, she asks him to abandon his realm and come with her. He replies, "You suggested that before, Nada. My answer has not changed. I have my responsibilities. I cannot abandon them" (Sandman 28:8). The offer, of course, is the one also given by Lucifer and Destruction, and it is one that will remain in Dream's mind.

The theme of freedom and responsibility exists throughout *Sandman*, but it is in the penultimate volume, "The Kindly Ones," that it comes to the fore. It begins when the Cluracan comes to bring Nuala back to Faerie. Dream says that "the palace staff are my responsibility," to which Cluracan replies "you are responsible for many things, sire" (Sandman 58:23). His early attitude towards responsibility is shown in "A Season of Mists," as "We do what we must, Lucien. Sometimes we can choose that path we follow. Sometimes our choices are made for us. And sometimes we have no choice at all" (Sandman 22:23).This early in the story, he has not yet realized the extent of his freedom, or his responsibility to himself. Later, Delirium comes to Dream while he is performing his duties. She is searching for her lost dog, given to her by Destruction, and she asks for Dream's help. He replies, "Sister, I have responsibilities. I cannot leave the Dreaming at this time." When she asks him to define his responsibilities, he answers, "Well, I use it to refer to that area of existence over which I exert a certain amount of control and influence. In my case, the realm and action of dreaming" (Sandman 64:8). Delirium tells him that he uses the word so much, and that there are other kinds of responsibility, for example, that "Our existence deforms the universe. That's responsibility." Indeed, one of the themes of myth is that despite the apparent smallness of our lives, each of our existences has effects on the universe we can only imagine. Delirium's speech is also the first indication we see of other types of responsibility, and it comes at a time when Dream's emotional life is beginning to spill over into his work. If he and the Dreaming are reflections of each other, then the Dreaming reflects his conflict, as in "The Kindly Ones" ravens start to gather in his realm, in anticipation of the great battle coming. This personal responsibility is above all a responsibility to himself. After all, he is of little use to the Dreaming if he performs his responsibilities at the expense of his (new-found) emotional life.

Another aspect of Dream's changing relationship with responsibility comes in his following of the rules. In issue 2, when he calls on the Grey Sisters, he says "this is my realm. It has laws. And the beings in the world conform to those laws" (Sandman 2:20). Later, we see that he follows many laws. In his final meeting with Thessaly, she has kept him from killing Lyta Hall, thus ending the threat against him and his realm. She has drawn a protective circle, but he says "I could kill her. There are many ways to end a human life. I could do it without breaking the circle." Thessaly answers "without breaking the circle, perhaps. But without breaking the *rules*?" He replies, " . . . no. I must do it myself, directly" (Sandman 65:21). Later, Matthew asks Dream why he does not just end the threat of the Furies. Dream tells him, "Because there are rules. And because they are part of something far huger and older than simple goddesses and bound and empowered by rules, as I am" (Sandman 68:3). Of this state, Robert Olson says that "fallenness is a state in which the individual constantly obeys commands and prohibitions whose source is unknown and unidentifiable and whose justification he does not bother to inquire into" (136). Of course, every god and goddess comes with rules, and Dream is of a mind to follow many of them.

However, in the end, he must face the fact that even following the rules is a choice, and a choice that, like everything else, he will be held responsible for. Niebuhr tells us that keeping the laws of a given system can still be a form of evil, as "the freedom of man is such that he can make keeping the law the instrument of evil" (II, 40). Thus, simply following the rules does not protect us. As Robert Olson says, "not to choose is also to choose, for even if we deliver our power of decision to others, we are still responsible for having done so. It is always the individual who decides that others will choose for him. At times he may dull the awareness of his original and inalienable responsibility, but he can never wholly suppress that awareness" (52). Olson continues this line of thought, that "even if God did exist and even if man could know God, nothing would be changed. Since man is free, he must choose his own values and take upon himself the responsibility for his choice. He cannot shift this responsibility to God" (87).

Dream decides to follow the rules of the Furies, above all the rule that blood-crimes must be avenged . . . with more blood. In dealing with the Furies, he decides to play a waiting game by not leaving the Dreaming. However, he is soon called away by Nuala (who ironically is trying to help him). He goes to her, and in doing so, dooms himself. It is important to realize, as he does not until later, that his going to her, too, was a choice, and one that he is responsible for. When he tells Death of the incident with Nuala, she rebukes him, "Don't you start blaming Nuala for this. You didn't *have* to do anything." He answers, "No . . . you are right, of course . . . It has nothing to do with Nuala. It has everything to do with me" (Sandman 69:6). At that point, there is little else that Dream can do, but only because this is what he really wants to do.

It is only at the end, however, that Dream finally takes responsibility for all the events recounted in "The Kindly Ones." Before he goes off to "fight" the Kindly Ones, he says, "Rules and responsibilities: these are the ties that bind us. We do what we do, because of who we are. If we did otherwise, we would not be ourselves. I will do what I have to do. And I will do what I must" (Sandman 67:24). Later, when Death comes to him, she brings him to task for everything that has happened. She says, "I've known you longer than anybody. You've been down much farther than this in the past, and you've come back. They took the Dreaming away from you, once, and you regained it. Remember? The only reason you've got yourself into this mess is because this is where you wanted to be." (Sandman 69:5). She finishes by saying "There's personal responsibility too, y'know? Not only the kind you're always talking about." After the exchange about Nuala, Dream admits that the choices that have led him to this point were his and his alone. "Since I killed my son . . . the Dreaming has not been the same . . . or perhaps I was no longer the same. I still had my obligations . . . But even the freedom of the Dreaming can be a cage, of a kind, my sister" (Sandman 69:6). Death brings up Destruction, and suggests that Dream could have left the Dreaming behind. However, he says, "No. I could not," and she puts her arm around his neck and says "No, you couldn't, could you?" If Dream could have left, then he would not have been himself. And as Lucien says in "The Wake," there are limits to how much Dream can change. Besides, to leave would (presumably) be to plunge the Dreamworld into chaos, such as the kind that occurred when he was imprisoned. Dream cares too much about his duties to simply abandon them, so he does the most responsible thing he can, which is also the only thing he can. His own status (what, were he mortal, we would call mental health) aside, when Dream takes his sister's hand, he is ensuring that the Dreaming will be taken care of. Daniel will be a more human Dream, and will perform his duties in a way Morpheus simply could not anymore. In this sense, the old Dream is being far more responsible in dealing with his problems than either Lucifer or Destruction. In the end, Dream takes personal responsibility over the kind he previously referred to.

Before we examine issues of freedom and responsibility throughout the series, we must first consider the cases of two characters we have already referred to: Destruction and Lucifer. Both are rulers who give up their kingdoms and responsibilities, and both have a chance to explain their decisions when they encounter Dream. Destruction abandoned his realm 300 years ago (so we are told) so that he would not have to preside through the period of great destruction on Earth that would follow the discoveries of Einsteinian physics ("the age of great explosions"). When Dream and Delirium find him, Dream asks what has become of Destruction's realm. He answers, "I'm sure it's still there, in its fashion. People and things are still created; still exist; are still destroyed. They tear down and they build. Things still change. The only difference is that no one's running it anymore. It's nothing to do with me any longer. It's theirs. They can make their own destruction. *It's not my responsibility. And it's not my fault*" (Sandman 48:8, emphasis mine). After the encounter, Dream seems to assume Destruction will return to his realm, because it is the right thing to do. When Destruction says he has no intention of doing so, Dream becomes flustered and says "But you are of the Endless. We . . . We have responsibilities. You are the embodiment of Destruction. You are of the Endless" (Sandman 48:15). Destruction responds with a speech that redefines our perception of the Endless: "The Endless? The Endless are merely patterns. The Endless are ideas. The Endless are wave functions. The Endless are repeating motifs. And even our existences are brief and bounded. None of us will last longer than this version of the universe . . . I filled my role more than adequately for over ten billion years. A two-sided coin: Destruction is needed.

Nothing new can exist without destroying the old" (Sandman 48:16). In a sense, Destruction's example may be a way of easing us into a new mode of thinking: one without gods and goddesses. Rather, the world seems to work without them. Of course, the example might not be totally appropriate, because of the nature of Destruction's realm. It seems that without the Endless, their realms fall into chaos (at least Dream's did when he was imprisoned). But in Destruction's case, chaos is exactly what made up his realm in the first place. Still, his example is there, for anyone to follow. Additionally, Destruction leaving his realm signifies the kind of large-scale, world-shaping change Gaiman refers to.

The other side of Destruction's leaving is that he offers that option to Dream as well. He says to his brother, "My brother. There is nothing I can give you, save this: my advice. Remember what I did. Remember that I left. Remember how hard it was for me to leave. And that it was not your fault" (Sandman 48:18). Later, at Morpheus's funeral, Destruction comes to Daniel, to see his new brother. He tells Daniel, "You know you could leave all this. It'll carry on all right without you. Come out with me and walk the stars. It's astonishing how much trouble one can get oneself into, if one works at it. And astonishing how much trouble one can get oneself *out of*, if one simply assumes that everything will, somehow or other, work out for the best" (Sandman 72:79). He adds later, "Entropy and optimism: the twin forces that make the universe go around." According to one view (Dream's original view), Destruction is being completely irresponsible: he is one of the Endless, and has abandoned his realm completely. However, one could also view his actions as following his own path. For who among us have not found themselves in a situation he or she did not want to be in? If relationships are one side of responsibility, then the other side is the way such attachments can trap us. For anyone who has been in an unpleasant job, or an intolerable family situation, walking away can be an act of great courage. Behind Destruction's carefree delivery is someone who gave up everything he had known for 10 billion years, and in this sense, he is irreducibly brave.

In a manner very similar to Destruction's abandoning his realm, Lucifer forsakes his as well. His action, though, also has repercussions for individuals' lives. When he hears of Dream's coming return to Hell, it crystallizes his plan to abandon his realm. When Dream does arrive, he finds Hell almost empty, as Lucifer is busy expelling its last inhabitants. As he tells Dream, "Yes, I rebelled. It was a long time ago. How long was I meant to pay for that one action? So now it's over. I have sent all of them away . . . I don't care where they've gone. Heaven. Earth. Limbo. The far realms. Who knows? But they won't be coming here any more. Hell is over" (Sandman 23:19). He also tells Dream: "perhaps this is the ultimate freedom, eh, Dreamlord? The freedom to leave . . ." (Sandman 23:20). Later, in the nightclub (appropriately titled "Lux" for light) he runs in Los Angeles, he tells Delirium, "I told him, you know. I told him years ago . . . I told him that I owed him much for having given me the impetus to go. I told him there was always freedom, even the ultimate freedom. The freedom to leave. You don't have to stay anywhere forever" (Sandman 68:14).

At the same time, Lucifer reveals something important about Hell: that people are there because they want to be. As he tells Dream, "Why do they blame me for all their little failings? They use my name as if I spend my entire say sitting on their shoulders, forcing them to commit acts they would otherwise find repulsive. 'The Devil made me do it.' I have never made one of them do anything. Never. They live their own tiny lives. I do not live their lives for them" (Sandman 23:18). He continues his speech, that "and then they die, and they come here (having transgressed against what they believed to be right), and expect us to fulfill their desire for pain and retribution. I don't make them come here. They talk of me going around and buying souls, like a fishwife come market day, never stopping to ask themselves why. I need no souls. And how can anyone own a soul? No. They belong to themselves . . . they just hate to face up to it" (Sandman 23:18). In *The Power of Myth*, Bill Moyers mentions a similar idea, taken from Campbell's writing, that "you wrote once that the point about hell, as about heaven, is that, when you're there, you're in your proper place, which is finally where you want to be" (191). Along with their lives, then, people have to take responsibility for their own afterlives. Each person's soul is his or her own, and no one can take that away. Thus, paradoxically, at the same time Lucifer abandons his responsibilities, he urges people to take responsibility for themselves. As we have seen, taking responsibility is one of the things *Sandman* is about.

Finally, with Lucifer, there is also the question of responsibility for his rebellion and Fall. Dream tells Lucifer that he was passionate in Heaven before the Fall. Lucifer replies, "I cared about so many things . . . I suppose that was why everything began to go wrong. You know . . . I still wonder how much of it He planned. How much of it He knew in advance. I thought I was rebelling. I thought I was defying His rule. No . . . I was merely fulfilling another tiny segment of His great and powerful plan" (Sandman 23:15). This intuition is shown to be correct in "Murder Mysteries," the one Gaiman short story that I consider to be part of the Sandman world. The story takes place in Heaven before the creation. In it, (pre-Fall) Lucifer is made to witness the destruction of an angel who killed another angel who he (or more appropriately, *it*) loved. After the destruction, Lucifer is seized by emotion, as "'That was not right,' he said. 'That was not just.' He was crying; wet tears ran down his face. Perhaps Saraquael was the first to love, but Lucifer was the first to shed tears" (Murder Mysteries, *Angels and Visitations*, 162). Later, it is revealed that God set up the situation so that Lucifer would witness an injustice on the part of the Lord, so as to push him on the path to the war against Heaven. God does this, we assume, because He needs an Adversary: someone to run Hell. As he tells the main character, "Lucifer must brood on the unfairness of Saraquael's destruction. And that—amongst other things—will precipitate him into certain actions. Poor sweet Lucifer. His way will be the hardest of all my children; for there is a part he must play in the drama that is to come, and it is a grand role" (Murder Mysteries 164). Aside from the story's revisionist interpretation of Lucifer's rebellion and fall (The Devil was set up!), it opens up the larger question of agency. For even though Lucifer's actions were manipulated by God, he still performed them, and as such is responsible for what he has done.

And in a way, he was taking responsibility for his own life when he decided to abandon Hell. As our religious traditions have lost their meaning for many of us, life as the Adversary did not hold the meaning it once did, so Lucifer had the choice of remaining in Hell as a shell of his former self, or of moving on, and making his peace with God. This peace can be seen in the end of "A Season of Mists," when Lucifer and the old man are on the beach. The old man tells Lucifer that, although he's lost everyone he loved, any God that could create the sunset, every night, couldn't be all bad. After the man leaves, Lucifer says (apparently to God): "All right. I admit it. He's got a point. The sunsets are bloody marvelous, you old bastard . . . Satisfied?" (*Sandman* 28:20). Thus, even Lucifer is able to come to terms with his past, once he takes responsibility for it. (As a side note, Vertigo has begun publishing a spin-off series, "Lucifer," about the continuing adventures of the former prince of darkness.)

Finally, if *Sandman* is to function as a myth, there is the question of what all this means for the reader. One possibility might be that if you find yourself in an intolerable situation, you can always walk away. Although the price may be high for doing so, there are few, if any, situations that you cannot get yourself out of if you are willing to do what is necessary. Which brings us back to freedom. And the price of freedom is that we must take responsibility for our lives, even if we have not been fully in control of them. The freedom to walk away might not be the ultimate freedom (as Lucifer suggests), but it is a considerable one. It is also possible to argue against free will in the *Sandman* universe. After all, Destiny carries a book that contains all our destinies, everything that will happen to us. When the wind blows, it ruffles the pages to the past . . . or to the future. However, to complain that one is not free to choose one's actions is to miss the point. In the end, your life must be your own. Some of us have more to overcome than others, but the sooner we accept our unique lives, the better off we are.

The inevitable other side to the idea of freedom is, of course, what we do with that freedom. That is, we are free, both to help people, or to hurt them. And thus freedom opens up consideration of the problem of evil. As we have said before, in *Sandman* there is no underlying logic to either violence or suffering, and no explanation given for the origin of evil, as some myths in the past have endeavored to do. This is because in modern life, we have seen and experienced things than cannot fit into the rubric of theodicy, and that we cannot possibly find a rationalization for. But while we must let go of attempts to explain the presence of evil in the world, we also must part with the idea that anyone is "pure evil." Instead, we see the world as being filled with people, each with their own issues and problems. And while it is true that many people make others suffer, to call that person "evil" is to miss the point, that the capacity for violence lurks in each one of us.

As an example, let us cite what is possibly the most famous study in social psychology, the Melgrim study. Melgrim recruited subjects, ostensibly for an experiment about learning word-pairs. They were told to read the words at certain times, and to administer electric shock to the learner, if he got them wrong (actually, there was no learner, only a recording). The subjects were then instructed to increase the voltage, while the recording played screams, as they thought the learners were crying out and begging him not to continue. The subjects were visibly shaken, but as long as the experimenter told them to continue, they continued to raise the voltage. Eventually, the voices stopped, but the experiment continued, as it was made to seem that the learner had been shocked into unconsciousness, or even death. Two thirds of the subjects followed the instructions up to the top level of shocks. Only one third of them refused to comply with the experimenter's wishes. When asked about this experiment, most people attribute the results to something evil or weak inside the subjects. The point that they miss is that it was not the subjects, but the situation that proved to be so powerful, and that people will basically do anything they are told to by someone in authority. The lesson to be learned here is that the situation can have a greater effect on the outcome of an event than the character of the people involved. At the trial of high-ranking Nazi official Adolf

Eichmann, reporter Hannah Arendt coined the phrase "the banality of evil": "the lesson of the fearsome, word-and-thought-defying *banality of evil*" (231, emphasis in original). She was expecting to find a monster, and instead found a small, old, bespectacled man. *This* was the man who once joked about killing six million Jews? What people do not realize, and the much harder lesson to learn, is that such a capacity lies within each of us, and we cannot displace blame onto the other. Arendt writes that "the trouble with Eichmann was precisely that there were so many like him, and that the many were neither perverted nor sadistic, that they were, and still are, terribly and terrifyingly normal" (253). Melgrim discusses Eichmann's trial, that "Arendt contended that the prosecution's effort to depict Eichmann as a sadistic monster was fundamentally wrong, that he came closer to being an uninspired bureaucrat who simply sat at his desk and did his job . . . Somehow, it was felt that the monstrous deeds carried out by Eichmann required a brutal, twisted, and sadistic personality, evil incarnate" (Melgrim 5-6).

What does this all have to do with *Sandman*? It involves agency. There are no demons, no entities of pure evil. As we have seen, even the Devil is a fairly sympathetic character. That is not to say there is no violence in the series. Like other myths (imagine the Trojan War), the series is filled with violence and suffering. However, if we look beneath the surface, we see only people (or gods—as it becomes almost impossible to differentiate people from gods). One approach to evil that might be effective here, instead of considering beings as wholly good or evil, is to view evil in terms of wrongdoing and suffering. Paul Ricoeur defines "blame" and "lament," as "there is blame where a human action held to be a violation of the prevailing code of conduct is declared guilty and worthy of being punished. There is lament where some suffering is undergone. We do not make it happen, it befalls us . . . whereas blame makes culprits of us, lament reveals us as victims" (Figuring the Sacred 250). Ricoeur also notes that "the ambivalence of the sacred, as described by Rudolf Otto, confers on myth the power to assume both the dark and the luminous sides of the human condition" (Figuring 251). In the face of such suffering, we have no recourse other than to turn it into a complaint, often against God. Ricoeur writes that "the emotional response . . . cannot be anything other than a catharsis of the emotions that nourish the lament and that transform it into a complaint" (Figuring 259). The complaint, then, is why do these things happen to us? As Ricoeur adds, "the arbitrary and indiscriminate way in which suffering is apportioned whether by violence or by the ultimate part of suffering that cannot be ascribed to interaction . . . keeps rekindling the old questions: not just Why? But Why me? Why my beloved child?"(Figuring the Sacred 259). Elsewhere, Ricoeur says that "suffering is not explained, ethically or otherwise" (Symbolism of Evil, 321). He also emphasizes that "a powerful incitement to questioning springs from suffering and sin: 'How long, O Lord?' 'Have I sinned against some divinity?' 'Was my act pure?' One might say that the problem of evil offers at the same time the most considerable challenge to think and the most deceptive invitation to talk nonsense" (Ricoeur, Symbolism of Evil 165).

In *Sandman*, I would argue that we see an example of lament and questioning in Rose Walker after she is almost killed in "The Doll's House." She also tells of trying to come to terms with her best friend Judy's death (that we saw in the diner in "24 Hours"—issue 6). Rose hardly leaves her room for six months, living a kind of shadow existence and brooding about the implications of what has happened to her. In a way, she is lamenting the loss of her innocence, and of her grandmother, Unity, as she asks not only "why?", but "why me?" And because, in the end, there can be no satisfactory answer to that question (as there is no reason given, for instance for the suffering and death in the diner—it merely happens), she eventually gives it up and rejoins the human race. Another illustration of this principle is when Matthew decides that he does not want to die, even though Morpheus is gone. He sums up the principle by saying, "Funeral's over. Time to get on with our lives. Time to grow up" (Sandman 72: 89). Here, Matthew reaffirms life, moving past his lament and rejoining the world of the living.

In *Sandman*, we encounter violence at all turns. However, it is interesting to note that there are few, if any, true *villains*, especially in a medium that thrives on stories of super-villains.

It is also an instructive example to ask who is responsible (there's that word again) for the central tragedy of the series, the death of Dream. Who (in effect) kills the Dream-Lord. The Furies? They are just doing their job of avenging blood-crimes. Loki? Perhaps, but he gets it worse than he gives (indeed, Loki ends up in one of the worst situations, not only being tortured by the snake, but losing his eyes to the Corinthian). Nuala? After all, she does force Dream to leave the Dreaming, but she was only trying to help. Lyta Hall? She was only trying to regain her son, in her own disturbed way. Thessaly? She was only looking our for herself (actually, Thessaly is the one character in the episode that I actually *blame*). No, in the end, it must be Dream that takes responsibility for his own death, as he eventually does.

To extend the exercise, however, we should ask if there are any other villains in the story. Roderick Burgess? He, after all, captures Dream in the first place. But he never profited from his action. Alex? He merely inherited a problem he did not want to deal with. The Corinthian? He was only acting according to his nature, as a dark mirror for humanity. Jed's abusive step-parents? They were manipulated by Brute and Glob. Dream? Aye, there's a conundrum. After all, he does consign Nada to Hell. And he leaves Orpheus to his fate (the first time), and traps Alex Burgess in an eternal nightmare. But as we have seen, one of the most moving parts of the series is watching Dream becoming human and trying to atone for his past misdeeds, deeds we still cannot ignore, however. And so on. We see, then, that even though there are characters who act wrongly and cause suffering, there are few, if any, cases of pure evil. Rather, there are simply responsible agents moving throughout their lives, who often cause others to suffer. And if you ignore the supernatural aspects, that is a fairly apt assessment of the world we live in.

However, there is an important exception to what I have said about evil. One of the functions of myth is to describe the types of evil that are out there, and Gaiman would be remiss if he were to ignore the decidedly modern twist we have put on evil. Put another way, there are things out there that can hurt you very badly, and the myth had better tell us about them. For the demons of today are represented by the serial killer. The issue

"Collectors" (issue 14) features a convention of serial killers. Although there is an undertone of dark humor throughout (especially with the "death" puns at the beginning), there are a few moments in which the killers are revealed to be human, just people who are as scared and frightened as the rest of us. Of course, the difference is that they choose to respond to these issues by killing people, while the rest of us do not. (Some of the killers are in fact torn and conflicted by what they do.)

The other notable theme in the issue is the romanticization of violence. We do, after all, live in a culture that has produced serial killer trading cards. As this was being written, a second movie about the fictional serial killer Hannibal Lechter was ending its theatrical run, in which it broke all kinds of box office records. More recently, a "prequel" cleaned up as well. As a culture, we hold some kind of morbid fascination about murderers, those who kill to kill. This romanticization can be seen clearly in the Corinthian's guest of honor speech, as "We are the American daydreamers, driving down the holy road to true knowledge that's paved with blood and gold. And across the length and breadth of this fair country, we are killing people. We don't do it to make a living. We don't do it for revenge. . . . We do not murder for a profit. We do not murder for governments, or for hire. We kill to kill. . . . We are gladiators, and we are soldiers of fortune, and we are swashbucklers and heroes and kings of the night" (Sandman 14:32-3). At the speech, Dream confronts his creation, puncturing the Corinthian's romantic view: "You disappoint me, Corinthian. You, and these humans you inspired and created, disappoint me. You were my masterpiece, or so I thought. A nightmare created to be the darkness, and the fear of darkness in every human heart. A black mirror, made to reflect everything about itself that humanity will not confront. But look at you. Forty years walking the earth, honing yourself, infecting others with your joy of death and what have you given them? What have you wrought, Corinthian? Nothing. Just something else for people to be scared of, that's all. You've told them that there are bad people out there. And they've known that all along" (Sandman 14:33). The Corinthian, in a way, served his purpose *too* well. The phenomenon of the serial killer may be a strictly modern one, but now it has been enshrined in a myth. And the lesson is that there are people out there who can hurt you, very badly. But perhaps we have known it all along, for to deny that one has in oneself the capacity to hurt someone that badly is to miss the point of the lesson. In the end, the face of evil is none other than ours.

At bottom, issues of freedom and responsibility provide a useful way of looking at *The Sandman*. As we have seen, the relative preponderance of rulers who forsake their kingdoms provides the gateway into the larger issue of our responsibilities to our fellow people. From Destruction and Lucifer, we learn that there is always the option of leaving, no matter how difficult that might prove. In particular, with Lucifer, we have the story of one who, although he may have been initially manipulated, takes control of his life in leaving his post behind. Also, we have the idea that we are responsible for our own souls, and that the only way we might end up in Hell is if we want to be there. Then there is Dream, who exhibits a greater commitment, and who ensures the continued ordered chaos of the Dreaming by preparing the way for the new Dream, one who will perform his duties much better than the old one.

At the same time, we have seen how such wide freedom can lead to the choice of evil, to cause suffering in the lives of others. And while the idea of pure evil may no longer be appropriate or even feasible, there remain people and things out there that can hurt us very badly. As followers of the Corinthian, serial killers may carry the role of "dark mirrors," but only if we displace the darkness inside us onto them. In the end, we can use Ricoeur's categories of blame and lament in order to decry the suffering undergone in our own lives, while trying to prevent suffering in the lives of others. And moving past one's own lament might be another important stage in "growing up" spiritually. Here again we are reminded of Campbell's fourth (psychological) function of mythology, as it moves us through the stages of our lives.

Finally, if *The Sandman* is filled with violence or the threat of violence, it is powerful because it also shows us the effects of violence, and the suffering it leaves in its aftermath. Robert Olson discusses the existentialists' tendency to "[master] the technique of reaffirming the value of life while boldly depicting its horrors" (2). This description fits *Sandman*, as the violence is presented with an unflinching quality; we see the violence, and its effects. When Judy is killed in the diner, we see Rose grieving her loss, and Foxglove having nightmares about her. When Wanda dies, Barbie goes cross-country to attend her funeral. And when Dream of the Endless dies, an entire volume of *Sandman* is devoted to the other characters' response to this loss. In this sense, here Gaiman is showing us the other side of the problem of death: the suffering undergone not only by the deceased, but by those close to him or her. And however we choose to deal with the problems and suffering in our life, in the end we are the only ones who can be truly responsible for our own lives.

FEARFUL SYNTHESIS: THE BLENDING OF THE OLD AND NEW IN *THE SANDMAN*

"One way to get the feeling back into thinking is to remythologize it, repeople it with Gods and Goddesses, so that the abstractions take on aesthetic concretion and the ideas may be reinvested with passion."

—Daniel Miller

"New Age? No, I'm afraid. Quite the opposite, really."

—Thessaly, also called Larissa

Up until now, we have been discussing *The Sandman* primarily in light of classic mythological themes: the importance of dreams, the hero's journey, and death and change. However, one could easily find these themes in the myths of just about any tradition, and we have yet to see what makes Gaiman's work a distinctly modern myth. Indeed, the term is somewhat paradoxical, since many of the features we normally associate with myth (traditional authorship, being shaped over centuries) do not apply to *Sandman*. Joseph Campbell and others have noted the difficulty in shaping a myth for the modern world. Campbell tells us that "life today is so complex, and it is changing so fast, that there is no time for anything to constellate itself before it's thrown over again" (Power 132). Still, this does not mean that we cannot, or should not, try. An especially perceptive artist could take a moment of the present and infuse it with mythological energy, and many have tried to harness the power of myths in their own (modern) stories. Still, one of the points that I have tried to argue is that only having mythological characters or elements does not make a myth. Rather, a certain depth of meaning and emotion is required to advance these narratives past the point of "creative postmodern storytelling." In the hands of a lesser talent, such works are usually mediocre at best. In the hands of one like Gaiman, the narrative truly rises to the level of myth, or even a mythology (a complete world of myth). And one key to the creation of the unique state of a modern myth is the synthesis of old and new elements, and the balance between them.

If *Sandman* contains elements of the old and new, one of the most important "new" elements is Gaiman's social vision. Gaiman's work includes an implicit sociology, and lays out principles for how we should treat each other. Equally significant is the inclusion of characters who have been, up until now, been left outside the mythological discourse: strong women outside the roles of wife and mother, and queer and transgendered characters. Gaiman also takes a stand in the fight against AIDS and the stigma it often brings; his stand, coming in the early 90's, is quite significant (and even a little revolutionary). Campbell lays out the sociological function as validating a certain social order; however myth can be used to challenge a given social order. In this way, *Sandman* is in parts closer to folklore than myth (although the two are notoriously difficult to separate), as folklore often challenges the ideologies of a society's myths. Gaiman uses folkloristic elements and includes characters from groups that have been marginalized by society, and by "traditional" myths. If the old morality of the established religions is no longer relevant or true, then it needs to be replaced with a new sensibility. The male, musclebound, hero and the beautiful, blonde damsel in distress do not translate well to the modern world. The theme of identity, then, is one we shall have to explore in the new context. And although the moments are somewhat less apparent than, say, the theme of dreams, they are present in the greater narrative.

Thus, one of the reasons that *Sandman* is a modern myth is that it exists equally in the spheres of old and new, ancient and modern, material. It features old gods in new situations, and new gods (or beings like gods) throughout the ages. In addition, Gaiman introduces a new pantheon, the Endless, who act much like a dysfunctional family. The series is also pluralistic, treating the myths and legends of diverse cultures with equal reverence, and even at times lets them interact. It features traditional mythological elements, like the hero's journey or myth's often earthy quality, and places them in new situations. For most of the old gods, the new situation is the modern spiritual dilemma; the loss of belief has hurt them just as much as it has hurt us.

First, let us turn to the social vision; the matter of social order is important. Campbell says, "the models have to be appropriate to the time in which you are living, and our time has changed so fast that what was proper fifty years ago is not proper today. The virtues of the past are the vices of today. And many of what were thought to be vices of the past are the necessities of today. The moral order has to catch up with the moral necessities of actual life in time, here and now. And that is what we are not doing. The old-time religion belongs to another age, another people, another set of human values, another universe" (Power 13). Later, he says "when the world changes, then the religion has to be transformed" (Power 21). Speaking specifically of the order endorsed by Christianity, he adds that "the story that we have in the West, so far as it is based on the Bible, is based on a view of the universe that belongs to the first millennium BC. It does not accord with our concept either of the universe or of the dignity of man" (Power 31). If the order is based over 2000 years ago, then it is no wonder that it is out of date. Of course, some aspects of myth are eternal, or at least long-lasting (why else would we continue to tell them?), but the social aspect of myth is one that ages more quickly, and for this reason we need new myths. It is also important to note that Campbell is fairly conservative on the social aspects of myth, saying that they validate a given social order. Other scholars of myth have pointed to ways in which it can serve as a challenge to the existing social order. Gaiman, I believe, fits more easily into the second category.

Other scholars have also noted the social aspects of myth. Bronislaw Malinowski viewed myth as "a part of activities which *do* certain tasks for particular human communities . . . Myths do not have an intrinsic meaning; their meaning is given by their home context or situation" (Strenski xi). Also, myths are "active parts of culture like commands, deeds, or guarantees, certifying that some sort of social arrangement is legitimate . . . They maintain the legitimacy of our social arrangements" (Strenski xvii). Malinowski observes that "the manner of telling a story and the way in which it was received . . . were quite as important as the text itself" (139). To this, Malinowski adds that "the core of all sound communal life has always been a strong, living faith" (131), and this is what has been missing from the modern world. Invariably, the values of a culture are transmitted through narratives, as "we find that every tenet of belief, every dogmatic affirmation, has a tendency to be spun out into a long narrative" (Malinowski 135). *Sandman* fits this criteria as well, as its entirety stretches over 2,000 pages. Finally, myth also serves as "a foundation for belief" (146). Finally, George Stroup adds that "the community's common narrative is the glue that binds its members together" (133). In a similar vein, Alan Dundes talks about "folk ideas:" "traditional notions that a group of people have about the nature of man, of the world, and of man's life in the world" (109). Again, we must not forget the often "fuzzy" boundary between myth and folklore. It would also be interesting, in a later study, for someone to examine the folkloristic elements of *Sandman* more fully, just as my primary focus has been on myth.

Because times have changed so much, a new social order is called for. In *Sandman*, there are a few instances of what such an order might be. In "A Game of You," Wanda, a pre-operative transsexual, is not allowed to walk the moon's road because "she" is a man (that is, biologically male). Wanda counters with: "well, that's something the gods can take and stuff up their sacred recta. I know what I am" (Sandman 35:19). This matter has provoked some controversy, as some have accused Gaiman of tacitly accepting the dominant ideology (saying that Wanda is a man). However, Gaiman has said that he always agreed with Wanda, that "Yes, the gods have their points of view; but in *Sandman*, those have no more validity than the point of view of anyone else, even that of the humblest character" (Bender 121). Thus, in this case, *the gods are wrong*. Clearly, what the gods do or think is not necessarily paramount. As Bender says, "one of the tale's morals is that, ultimately, no one gets to define who you are but you" (115).

We can also see the clash of ideologies at Wanda's funeral. Her parents cut her hair, put her in a suit, and bury her under her given name of "Alvin." Wanda's aunt Dora, who is billed as one of the more tolerant members of the family, says at one point, "God gives you a body, it's your duty to do well by it. He makes you a boy, you dress in blue, he makes you a girl, you dress in pink. You musn't go trying to change things" (Sandman 37:14). Wanda's mother is even worse: "The hurricane. It was God's judgement of a city of sinners" (37:16). Still, Barbie has the last laugh, as she writes "WANDA" in pink lipstick over Wanda's grave, subverting the old order. This gesture is one of the little, defiant, loving gestures that make *The Sandman* so powerful. After writing on the tombstone, Barbie also gives the previously mentioned "secret worlds" speech, which could mean that we each carry entire worlds within us, worlds in which we can choose who we are and what we want to do. It is with a sad note that Gaiman's writing here has been true to life, as friends of transsexuals he knew have told him how the parents of a loved one tried to change his or her appearance back to the original gender. As Hollis says once, "All versions of the myth are true" (121). Confirmation of this theme came later in 1999, when Hillary Swank won the Academy Award for best actress for her portrayal of Brandon Teena (born Teena Brandon) in the movie "Boys Don't Cry." In her acceptance speech, Swank thanked "Brandon Teena." Teena's mother objected to this, making reference to her "daughter's" life, and saying that Swank had no right to mention "her." All versions of the myth are true.

The overall message of "A Game of You," it seems, is that we can even choose our genders, if we so desire. Here, the "new" morality is contrasted with the established Christian one, albeit a caricatured view of it (as few Christians, Pat Robertson and company excepted, would really believe that a hurricane was God's judgement on a city of sinners). For the new sociology, other parts of *Sandman* come to mind as well. At the end of "The Kindly Ones," Rose is talking to Hal about how Zelda and Chantal were "innocent," because they contracted AIDS through a blood transfusion. Hal responds, "Rosalita . . . there isn't any innocent. There isn't any guilty. There's just dead" (Sandman 69:18). The lesson here is that if we feel more sorry for someone who dies from AIDS contracted from a blood transfusion than for someone who contracts it sexually or through drugs, then we are implicitly buying into the ideology that the rest of the people who die from AIDS did something to deserve it. Of course, this is exactly what many "Christians" said in the early stages of the AIDS epidemic, and it has no place in the new morality. Gaiman, then, is advocating a new order.

For this reason, Gaiman has taken another stand on the issue of AIDS: this time, to try to prevent its spread. The relevant material is a short, six-page tract entitled "Death Talks about Life" found at the end of the "Death: the High Cost of Living" trade paperback. The content of the tract is fairly standard for a reader familiar with safe-sex literature such as the kind you would encounter in a health class: Death tells the reader what AIDS is, how one can get it, and how to use a condom. In fact, it is so innocent-looking that one might simply gloss over it; reading it in 1998, I certainly did. However, the passage is significant for a few reasons. First, Gaiman is taking a stand to try to prevent AIDS from spreading further. The placement would seem natural, as young people (the implied audience of comics) are especially at risk for the disease, but is in itself revolutionary. When it was written, in the early 90's, AIDS was hardly talked about, or if it was, people seemed to paint its victims as somehow deserving of the disease. For a while, fear and homophobia kept people from discussing the disease, and I would argue that Gaiman's stand, which he admits at the beginning might be controversial, urges people to make themselves safer from the disease. Thus, while the specifics of the tract might not be revolutionary, the fact that it exists at all is. The sociological function of myth can be to challenge the existing social order; here, Gaiman has thrown his weight behind safe sex activism.

Finally, *Sandman* transgresses social boundaries by containing an unusually large number (prior to more mainstream acceptance) of queer or transgendered characters: Wanda, Hazel & Foxglove, Hal, Paul & Alex, Jack, Zelda & Chantal, and Judy. Their inclusion is, or at least was at the time, controversial in a medium that used to appeal primarily to adolescent males. (It is important to note that the second Death miniseries—the story of Hazel and Foxglove—won an award from the Gay and Lesbian Alliance Against Defamation (GLAAD) for "positive portrayals of gay and lesbian characters" (Bender 124).) In "The Time of Your Life," as in "A Game of You," marginal characters are placed at the center of the story. In addition, Hazel and Foxglove have perhaps the most loving and fulfilling relationship in the series; they also receive the "happily ever after" ending. Of course they have their problems, but we see them working through them, and it remains apparent that they truly love each other. The message here might be that in order to regain relevance, myths must address people from walks of life outside the traditional societal mainstream, that the "brave hero gets the girl" pattern is not enough. Of course, in the world of comics, even having non-stereotypical female characters is somewhat rare, another lesson might be the importance of including women—*real* women (if many of our myths are androcentric). The moments of sociology are somewhat hard to find, as Gaiman rarely flat-out tells people how to live (except in "Death Talks about Life"), but we can see glimpses of a new social order. There is in *Sandman* a sense of individual dignity and worth to every human being. This is clearly visible in Barbie's "secret worlds" speech. When Barbie appears in "The Doll's House" with her husband Ken, she seems completely boring. In "A Game of You," however, we learn that there is so much more to her, that she contains within her secret worlds. Barbie is marginal because of our stereotypes—we look at her (at first) and see a vacuous blonde (named "Barbie," no less). In seeing Barbie as a rich, three-dimensional character, Gaiman affirms human worth and dignity, as the series fulfills the third, sociological function of myth.

In addition, it would be interesting to examine the role of gender in *The Sandman*. And while I will merely scratch the surface, a reader with more background in the subject could throw much light on the matter. In her introduction to *The Feminist Companion to Mythology*, Carolyne Larrington refers to myths "at the centre of a web of meanings" (xi), some of which are sociological. Rosemary Guiley refers to the idea of female divinity as "She of a Thousand Names" (417). This characterization in similar to the recurring Triple Goddess in *Sandman*, who encompasses aspects of countless female divinities, including the Fates, the Furies, the Grey Sisters, Eve, and some off the series' human characters, most notably Thessaly, Hazel, and Foxglove. Guiley also refers to the ritual of "Drawing Down the Moon," "in which the high priestess invokes the Goddess force into her and becomes a channel for that divine energy" (420). She also refers to the witches of Thessaly, "who were renowned and feared for their magic," because they could draw down and control the moon. It is no accident that the witch Thessaly (named for her former residence) is able to do just this, and that she appears in "A Game of You," the most female-centered story-line in the series. Thessaly, whatever we think of her, is a very strong woman, who can take care of herself and has survived for thousands of years. (Actually, she is more dangerous than some demons I know.) Finally, Jane Caputi speaks of the feminist movement of leading a quest "to reclaim that symbolizing / naming power" that has been stolen from them by a patriarchical system (425). A perfect example of this in *Sandman* is Wanda's right to be a woman, and Barbie's defiant writing on her tombstone. This discussion has of necessity been rather cursory, but I would like to mark this area as one for future study.

In sum, there are elements of an implicit social vision within *Sandman* that could be seen as fulfilling Campbell's third function of myth. Through the contrast between Barbie and Wanda's relatives, from the discussion between Hal and Rose, and from the wealth of gay/lesbian/queer/ transgendered characters, we can see a new way of being good, of being *human*, to each other.

Sandman contains an implicit sociology, and in this sense it is modern and new (advocating a new social order). However, in crafting the modern myth, the new is only given power if it is balanced with the old. And few scholars have understood the tension between the old and the new like David Miller, in his work *The New Polytheism*. Miller tells us that in order for us to achieve spiritual wholeness, the next step in our spiritual evolution must be a return to, and a revival of, polytheism. He says that our modern society is pluralistic in nature, and that "the multiple patterns of polytheism allow room to move meaning-fully through a pluralistic universe" (Miller ix). He tells of teaching a course in Greek mythology: "that is where I first noticed [the gods and goddesses'] reality and potency" (Miller viii). At the same time, he began to notice the decline of modern spirituality, and writes that "the death of God gives rise to the rebirth of the gods. We are polytheists" (Miller 4). Thus, rather than evoking despair, the modern dilemma is an opportunity to rediscover the vitality of mythic narratives that have been out of sight for hundreds of years, but never fully out of mind. He later tells us that "Gods and Goddesses are alive and well" (51). To this, Gaiman would probably add: but they need our help, as indeed many of the old gods are in danger of dying out. The pluralistic tendency is necessary, Miller argues, in a time in which "equally real, but mutually exclusive aspects of the self" exist, and that "Personal identity cannot seem to be fixed. Normalcy cannot be defined" (5). According to Miller, monotheistic thinking is one-dimensional. In contrast, polytheism provides "the paradigms and symbols that allow us to account for, to express, and to celebrate those multiple aspects of our reality that otherwise would seem fragmented and anarchic" (7). Many have spoken of the modern human condition as a loss of center, a condition both frightening and disheartening. Miller, however, counters that "after the fright passes, one notices a new sense of liberty: how everywhere one stands is a center, a new center, and the universe of meaning is not limited to a tight little horizon, a vicious circle of a single mind and lifetime" (11). He adds that "Polytheism is not a historical or an academic matter. It is a feeling for the deep, abiding, urgent and exciting tension that arises when, with a radical experience of the plurality of both social and psychological life, one discovers that a single story, a monovalent logic, a rigid theology, and a confining morality are not adequate to help in understanding the nature of real meaning" (11). Again, we see the theme that myth has to grab one somewhere deep, *below* the consciousness, in order to be effective. For Miller, the path is clear, and it leads back to the gods.

According to Miller, monotheism has failed us in that it allows only one mode of thinking, only one center. In particular, monotheistic theology is lacking; "it would seem inevitable that the God of a monotheistic theology would die, that he would suffer an ineluctable demise. The imperialism of the mind, like that of Prometheus' Zeus, cannot forever endure without the resource of life that comes from feeling and intuition. The mind simply cannot account for all of life. By itself it is finally impotent" (Miller 26). In addition, theologians have tried to monopolize the theological discourse. Miller also says that "*Any thinking and speaking about ultimate matters of human meaning and being is theologia.* The implication is that all men are theologians, and the sooner *professional* theologians learn this, the richer our theologizing will be" (Miller 28). Miller's contempt for theologians, especially monotheistic theologians, is clear. Of course, theology about a single God is not necessarily one-dimensional, as is shown by examining the rich theological traditions of Judaism, Islam, and Christianity. Miller seems to reject monotheistic theology on the grounds that it is *boring*, as "professional theology, like mononucleosis, just makes one tired" (46). Still, we need not throw out his entire argument. Where he may have a point is in wanting to return to the vitality of polytheistic religion as a model for our pluralistic society. For Miller, the matter hinges on "*whether the ancient stories of the gods and goddesses enable us to put a little life, a little feeling, back into Western thinking*" (13, emphasis mine). Later, he writes: "not only does polytheistic thinking give us impersonal and collective leverage on life's pluralistic meaning through stories of Gods and Goddesses, but it helps us to differentiate the polytheistic quality of each of the aspects of our plurality. This gives polytheistic thinking not only a breadth for our pluralisms but also a depth, a resonance, a religious quality that is characterized by its transcendent function" (69). We shall see how he lays out his challenge.

Part of Miller's argument hinges on the need for stories. Of course, we have been living with the narrative of Christianity for 2000 years, and there are some who would say that its time has passed, that it is no longer relevant. Miller says that "the thing that intellectuals and professional theologians can learn from 'the people' is that thinking, including thinking about

God, or about Gods and Goddesses, is polytheistic. This means that a polytheistic theology which corrects our Western mono-theistic theologizing will consider the stories of the Gods, told in concrete images, to be fundamental to the task of theology." From this point of view, myth can be seen as an essential part of theology. Campbell tends to place myth and religion as opposites of each other (see *The Power of Myth*, 141), but perhaps here the two can be reconciled, with myth playing an important part in an intact religious system. Miller continues with his idea, that "narrative theology may be the only way in our time to revivify an ir-relevant doctrinal theology which has abstracted itself out of life by managing to kill God. Concrete images make for a theology of the imagination and an imaginative theology" (Miller 29). The idea of a "theology of the imagination" is an important one. As we will see later, it is the duty of the artists among us to shape the new myths. Miller says that "religion means being gripped by a story" (30). Again, a narrative theology is key, as "our modern thinking is dead because it lacks the excitement and compellingness that a story can stir in man. He also says that *"one way to get the feeling back into thinking is to remythologize it, repeople it with Gods and Goddesses,* so that the abstractions take on aesthetic concretion and the ideas may be reinvested with passion" (33-4, emphasis mine). The answer, then, is remythologization.

According to Miller, once you become gripped by a story, you will be transformed. He says, "if you are deeply gripped by a story, so that it becomes a pattern and paradigm for your entire life, it is inevitable that you will think and speak about that story, even if only to yourself. You will theologize" (43). From per-sonal experience, I can assert that *Sandman* is capable of doing this, of becoming a part of your life, even a part of you, that you always consult.

Miller also speaks of past creators, as "Homer was compelled by one story, and then another, and then another, and so on, and he wrote a novel, an epic, a narrative: a story of the stories. Hesiod was likewise seized, and he wrote a poem, a song, a group of lyrics: a song of songs. Aeschylus was also moved, and he wrote a trilogy of plays: the drama of dramatic actions. To tell a story, to sing a song, to enact a drama—these too are *theologia*" (43). This point is also important, because one way of viewing *Sandman* is as a story *about* stories. We will return to this point in a later section, but in many places, Dream moves into the background, and it is the act of telling stories that is showcased, and shown to be absolutely vital. Later, Miller says that "a polytheistic theology will be a theology of story and narrative" (75).

In the modern world, then, it is polytheism that can transform us. Miller brings up the practice of depth psychology and psychotherapy, which we last encountered in the "dreams and myth" section, as a modern solution to our dilemma. He says that "if theology is two thousand years of faith seeking understanding, psychotherapy is two thousand years of understanding seeking life" (Miller 52). Psychotherapy, then, is another avenue of revivification. And depth psychology may be a way back into myth. Miller says that "Freud named one of our many imaginal fantasy structures by the name Oedipus. Presumably that is just the beginning. We enact many myths in the course of our lives. We feel deeply the configurations of many stories. We are the playground of a veritable theater full of Gods and Goddesses" (55). (Thus, Freud's use of myth is appropriate, but too narrow and uniform.) Miller also speaks of the gods as needing us, as "What do the Gods and Goddesses want with us? Our task is to incarnate them, become aware of their presence, acknowledge and celebrate their forms, so that we may better be able to account for our polytheism" (55). Whatever we think of Miller's argument, there is no disputing his enthusiasm, as he tells us that "the stories of the Immortals are a joy because they are splendid, concrete, powerful, yet real, personal, and full of feeling" (56). Speaking of the theology of the new polytheism, he says "it is lived in one's deepest feelings" (65). He adds that "the task begins in feeling and intuition, rather than in thinking" (72). Thus, it is not with our minds, but with our hearts, and our guts, that we seek to encounter the new old religious experience. And one can do few better things for theology and religion than injecting some life back into it.

Miller also argues that modern society has become too pluralistic to adopt a single model of functioning. He says that "a

polytheistic theology will be a phenomenology of all religions"
(72). Miller says that Greek polytheism in particular will be more
compelling than others. However, there is no reason his argument cannot be extended to other pantheons as well. And as we
will see, it is difficult to be more pluralistic than *Sandman*. Also,
Miller, despite any reservations we may have about his argument, captures a quality missing from many analyses of myth:
enthusiasm. It is what makes Campbell so compelling, even if
some of his formulations were too hastily made. With Miller, as
with Campbell, one gets a feeling from reading their work that
they truly *enjoyed* what they were doing. Miller says that "laughter is indeed one of the aims of this book—not literal laughter so
much as the liberation that comes from a comic release, or, in a
Shakespearean tragedy, from comic relief" (78). As we will see,
laughter is an important element in *Sandman*. Also, Miller has
reverence for the Gods, saying at one point that "they are the em-
powering worlds of our existence: the deepest structures of reality" (80). Again, the theme of depth enters into the picture.
Finally, another reason for the long discussion of Miller is that
he says "a polytheistic theology will be a theology of hope" (73).
As I have tried to argue (and will return to later), the stories told
in *Sandman* are stories of hope. At the end, no matter what happens, there is hope. He says that "the death of God is also *not* the
death of some more basic stories; it is the opposite. It is the possibility of the rebirth of deeper stories" (82). The death of the Western, monotheistic God does not spell the end of religion per se;
rather, we must find the old stories that, to our surprise, have
not lost their vitality. Likewise, the Death of Dream brings about
a revification of the Dreaming.

If *Sandman* blends old and new elements, Miller's argument, serves as an introduction to the "old." Of course, there are
also others. Many traditional mythic patterns are found in the
stories. We have already examined the hero myth, the personification of death, and the connection to dreams, but there are
more. There is more than a little truth to James Hollis's statement "it is not New Age but Old Age, as old as the archetypes"
(80). There is a parallel statement in "A Game of You," in which
Hazel asks Thessaly if she is doing something new age and she

responds "New Age? No. Quite the opposite, really" (Sandman 34:13). Much of *Sandman* is traditional, as old as myth. There is the "wise old man" figure, sometimes Dream but more often Gilbert. There is the triple goddess, the archetypal Maiden, Mother, and Crone. In traditional forms, this triad appears as the Weird Sisters, the Fates, and the Kindly Ones. However, other characters approximate the trio, most notably in "A Game of You." When Thessaly (crone), Hazel (mother), and Foxglove (maiden) enter the moon's road, they take on the identities of the three-who-are-one. Other examples of the trio take place in "The Kindly Ones" (Rose and the women playing draughts), and the three female victims of John Dee's terror in "Twenty-Four Hours" (issue 6). Indeed, one could make an interesting study of the role of female divinity in *Sandman*. The important thing to note here is that the old pattern is re-enacted by modern participants. Finally, there is the constant bickering between members of the Endless, who act in much the same way as the old Greek and Roman gods did. Again, the old pattern is given new life.

Another "traditional" element is the trickster figure, a pattern that exists across cultures. Again, we see folkloristic elements in the series, including the presence of tricksters, and in the use of humor throughout the text. In some ways, Desire is a trickster, although perhaps this role could be spread out among the three youngest Endless (Desire, Despair, and Delirium), as they are always challenging each other and playing power games. But most interesting are the already existing tricksters. And *Sandman* has two tricksters par excellence: Loki and Robin Goodfellow. It is Gaiman's visionary touch to get them together; naturally they hit it off right away. And they are not content just to wreak havoc in their own worlds; they kidnap Daniel and help trigger the events that lead to the death of Morpheus. Jung discusses the roles of the trickster, "his fondness for sly jokes and malicious pranks, his powers as a shape-shifter, his dual nature, half animal, half divine, his exposure to all kinds of tortures . . ." (Archetypes 255). This description fits Loki almost exactly. In Norse lore he turns into a salmon, or a bird, in *Sandman* he turns into an approximation of Daniel, the Corinthian, and fire. He tells dirty jokes, both in old myths and here. He fathers Fenris the wolf, and sends a wolf after the Corinthian and Matthew. Finally, he is tortured, not only by the snake in the cavern (traditional tale), but he incurs great damage at the hands of the Corinthian, losing both his eyes and having his neck broken (Sandman 55:12-13). Thus, the old form takes on new life (both the old form and new life are important).

Another traditional facet of folklore and myth that receives new life in *Sandman* is its inherent humor and earthiness. Campbell says that "humor is the touchstone of the truly mythological as distinct from the more literal-minded and sentimental theological mood. The gods as icons are not ends in themselves" (Hero with a Thousand Faces 180). In *The Power of Myth*, he adds that "a key difference between mythology and our Judeo-Christian religion is that the imagery of mythology is rendered with humor. You realize that the image is symbolic of something. You're at a distance from it" (220). Of course, Gaiman would probably add that sometimes the gods *can* be an end in themselves, but the key feature here is the importance of humor. And although it is often subtle or slight, humor is important in *Sandman*. Most prominent is the story Loki tells to Robin Goodfellow while they burn away Daniel's mortality, which, if not for its length, would be reproduced here. It ends with Thor hugging a squirrel and saying "You're ugly, you're hairy, and you're covered in shit. But you're mine and I love you!" (59:2-3). Indeed, folklore (perhaps more so than myth) is commonly earthy, even scatological. Miller makes a point about the earthiness of myth. To look at the gods as illusions or metaphors would be to lose this quality.

Also, there is Merv Pumpkinhead, who serves as the unofficial comic relief of the Dreaming. He is a "blue-collar" figure responsible for the physical attributes of the Dreaming, and he is always getting into trouble by talking about Dream, while Dream materializes behind him. Here, the humor is more formal than funny; it reminds one of an old vaudeville routine, or perhaps more appropriately, to the comic relief in a Shakespeare tragedy ("The Kindly Ones" is in many ways a tragedy). Merv also serves the function of letting the reader know when Dream is acting like a flake, and in this role he is an essential counterpart to Dream's adolescent brooding (see Sandman 60: 21-23). In addition, the sequence with Hector Hall as the "other" Sandman is humorous, but it takes the form of a parody of "cheesy" comics. It is important to note that there actually *was* a title like this in the 70's; this title really serves as a parody of itself. And most important for this scene is the fact that it makes Dream laugh, the only time he does so in the series (Sandman 12:17-8). The scene in "A Season of Mists" in which Thor propositions Bast (26:3), is not only funny, but quite appropriate, given Thor's temperament. Finally, there is the most subtle and humorous slam aimed towards Freud, perhaps because of (or in spite of) his reductive view of myth. When Dream takes Rose flying in the end of "The Doll's House," Rose says "Say, whoever you are. Do you know what Freud said about dreams of flying? It means you're really dreaming about having sex." Dream then offers the very sensible reply "Indeed? Tell me, then, what does it mean when you dream about having sex?" (Sandman 15:22). Also, the scene where Matthew tries to tell Delirium how to drive is filled with an almost slapstick quality. Thus, although it is a serious work, *The Sandman* is not without its moments of laughter.

Another synthesis of old and new elements is the role of the gods we encounter in the story. The gods, however, are placed in modern situations. For most of them, the modern situation consists of what we have been discussing: the modern spiritual decline. Most of the gods have felt this tendency as harsh, as their supply of believers has diminished. Many gods have died. Others have adapted. The ancient Japanese pantheon has been one to adapt, as Susano-O-No-Moto tells Dream, "We are expanding—assimilating other pantheons, later gods, new altars and icons. Marilyn Monroe is ours now, as are King Kong and Lady Liberty" (Sandman 26:18). This statement is important not only because it shows gods adapting to the new circumstances, but also because it gives a hint of how new gods and goddesses can be born and incorporated. Many scholars speak of the "myth of America"—this may be the current form myth has taken. Another important figure is Pharamond, who says he owes his life to Dream. Later, Dream explains to Delirium,

"He used to be a God. When we last met, in Babylon, his sacrifices were dwindling, and many of his shrines had already been abandoned. I merely suggested that he find himself a new occupation" (Sandman 43:21). Delirium responds "Oh. I didn't know you could stop being a god," to which Dream answers "You can stop being anything." Here, the important lesson is that even the gods are not invariant; rather they are subject to the same kind of radical change we all are (see the section on mortality and change). When times change, they too must change, or else die. We have already encountered the idea of gods as magnified dreams; this is merely the brutal reality of that statement, that gods exist only as long as there are people to believe in them. A second implication of Dream's statement is that if you can stop being anything, you can even cease to be one of the Endless, as Destruction did. The possibility that Dream could escape his situation by giving up his post does not occur to him at the time.

Two divinities who have an especially difficult time with the modern decline of spirituality are Ishtar and Bast. We have seen that many people have turned away from religion; such a movement is bound to impact the gods as well as humans. Ishtar (also known as Astarte and by a host of other names) has gone from a love goddess, where "the last time I danced, they had temples to me. Fifty priestesses in each temple" (Sandman 45:20), to an exotic dancer who uses what little worship she can get in order to survive. Again we see the inclusion of marginalized characters, as for part of "Brief Lives," a group of strippers are made central. Gaiman writes them, as with his other characters, with humanity: Tiffany is just trying to make a living. One of them has a Master's Degree in Women's Studies, and objects to the implication that she is in the "sex industry." Ishtar tells Dream, "this is all the temple I've got, and we're kind of short on oracles" (45:19). Equally sad is the story of Bast, the Egyptian cat-goddess. After Dream speaks with her, she awakes and sends a mangled cat an easy death, as "The effort tires her. She remembers when the prayers and offerings swarmed around her at all times, uncountable, when she would pick and choose between them . . . She is beginning to be scared of dreams. Bast is getting old" (Sandman 46:15). Bast does appear at Dream's funeral, but we do not know what happens to her after that. But the prospects for old gods and goddesses do not look good.

In addition to putting old gods into new situations, *Sandman* is also pluralistic in the ways Miller said of the "new polytheism." In featuring members of so many mythologies (Greek and Roman, Egyptian, Norse, Japanese, Jewish and Christian, and Farerie, to name a few), Gaiman is telling us that they are all equally valid. Each one is a product of human consciousness, and thus each one shares in the importance that holds. Campbell presents the idea that each mythology has acted with a defined out-group, upon whom aggression and hatred could be focused. However, we have reached the point where there is no out-group any more, that "there were formerly horizons within which people lived and thought and mythologized. There are now no more horizons. And with the dissolution of horizons we have experienced and are experiencing collisions, terrific collisions, not only of peoples but also of their mythologies" (Myths to Live by 254). In *Sandman*, we get to see these collisions, such as in "A Season of Mists," when the deities of so many mythologies actually interact. As Campbell says, "today there are no boundaries. The only mythology that is valid today is the mythology of the planet—and we don't have such a mythology" (Power 22). We may not have had one when Campbell wrote, but just a few years later, we do. Campbell also says that "we need myths that will identify the individual not with his local group but with the planet" (Power 24). Gaiman might not include representatives from *every* pantheon, but his integration of different gods, goddesses, and assorted mythological beings, as well as his inclusion of marginal (or liminal) characters, is a start. In this context, it is becoming easier to see what makes *Sandman* a *modern* myth.

Then there are the elements in *Sandman* that are completely new. First, of course, there are the Endless. Gaiman has crafted a mythology out of whole cloth, a mythology that explains why we *have* myths, because the Endless are the constituent elements of consciousness (as myths are formed out of consciousness). The Endless exist above and *behind* all gods, yet they also take on the aspects of gods. Still, in keeping with the synthesis of old and new, they are as old as time itself, older than any of the gods. Also, for all their modern dress, they behave in a manner familiar to us because it characterizes so much of Greek mythology. The Endless, upon examination, resemble nothing so much as a dysfunctional family—one without any parents, of course. Again, this aspect of the story resembles folklore. One example of this comes at the beginning of "A Season of Mists," as in the exchange between Dream and Desire: "I do not want a grape," "I could make you want one" (Sandman 21:15). The relationships between the Endless center on the conflict between the younger and older members, with Desire, Despair, and Delirium constantly challenging the others (except for Death, of course). At the family gathering, after Dream storms out, Death says to Desire, "Shut up, Desire. If you ever want to speak again . . . shut up" (21:19). Death usually stays out of the sibling rivalry, but perhaps it is her role to keep some sense of order on the scene. Of course, in the next scene she finds herself defending what Desire said to Dream. Much earlier (chronologically), during the Emperor Norton affair, Desire vows: "He wants subtle? He'll get subtle. Just watch me. Not here. Not with Norton. But I'll make him spill family blood, I'll bring the Kindly Ones down on his blasted head" (31:21). That is exactly what Desire tries to do in "The Doll's House," and of course Dream eventually spills family blood when he kills Orpheus, although it is not Desire's doing. However, after the fateful incident, Desire (in perhaps its only real moment of humanity in the series), admits that it is scared and grips Despair's hand (49:10). In a sense, the family disputes among the Endless are at the nexus of myth and folklore.

Gaiman also used established figures of myth and integrates them into his own framework. For example, he takes the Orpheus myth almost exactly from the ancient sources, except for his father (Dream, not Apollo), and his ultimate fate (that he survives being torn apart). Also drawing on the ancient sources (and reinforcing the theme of change), Gaiman references Ovid, as "Omnia mutantur, nihil interit." (Sandman 74:143). One translation of Ovid's passage reads "Everything changes; nothing dies; the soul Roams to and fro, now here, now there, and takes

What frame it will . . ." (XV, 161-8). Gaiman quotes the passage more poetically as "Everything changes, but nothing is truly lost." The quotation comes in one of the epilogue stories, and perhaps here, Gaiman is telling us that the old Dream is never completely gone as long as we remember him, and that a part of him lives on in Daniel. Thus, Gaiman appropriates for his own purposes figures from the world of myth, while at the same time providing an explanation of why myths exist (as the gods exist because of humans, and the Endless—humans' dreams and belief shape the gods, while the Endless exist *behind* the gods).

The synthesis of old and new elements is a wide-ranging category, but important because it gets at the idea of the modern myth. We have covered a wide area of ground. First, we have examined what Campbell called the sociological function of myth. However, instead of validating a given social order, Gaiman critiques it and shows us a new way of being good, being *human*, to each other (remember that one of the key elements to being human is relationality). And from Malinowski, we know that myth cannot be separated from its cultural context, and its communal life. *Sandman* also includes characters who have normally been excluded from enshrinement in myth (ie queer and transgendered characters), and places its characters in non-traditional roles. It also addresses the social issues of the day, especially the AIDS crisis; here, Gaiman makes a direct attempt to help the problem criticizing the reluctance of some to embrace safe-sex awareness (those who say abstinence is the only way and then look down on those who fall prey to diseases). And although advocating safe sex is relatively uncontroversial and safe now, at the time Gaiman was writing, the principle was not as well-accepted.

If the sociology of *Sandman* is the new, then other aspects of the series embody the tension between old and new. We have seen Miller and his theory that the next step in humankind's spiritual evolution will be a return to polytheism. It is also important to note that Miller equates what he calls the death of God with our modern spiritual dilemma. And regardless of the validity of his argument, we can take from it that idea that our society has become radically pluralistic, and that the old ways of thinking will not hold. This is what Campbell had in mind when he said that there are "no more horizons." In addition, *Sandman* is filled with traditional elements, such as the trickster figures, the Triple Goddess, and the earthy quality of myth. All of these elements point to the mythic (and folkloristic) quality of Gaiman's work. But where *The Sandman* really takes on the attributes of myth is where Gaiman introduces new elements, putting old gods into new situations. The synthesis of old and new is also visible in his conception of the Endless: a new set of beings that are very old, and behave just like the Greek gods of old. This is Gaiman's own myth, the myth of the Sandman. There is, however, another element of *Sandman* that embodies the tension between the old and new in the modern myth. It involves the way myth itself is produced, by the work of the individual artists and storytellers. For not only does *Sandman* exist as a story, but it also features as central characters storytellers and artists. It is these people (Gaiman included, of course) who are responsible for shaping the modern myth. Let us go on, then, and examine the role of the artist in shaping myth.

THE ROLE OF THE ARTIST AND THE ART OF STORYTELLING IN *THE SANDMAN*

"Myth must be kept alive. The people who can keep it alive are artists of one kind or another. The function of the artist is the mythologization of the environment and the world"

—Joseph Campbell

"I learned that we have the right, or the obligation, to tell the old stories in our own ways, because they are our stories, and they must be told"

—Neil Gaiman

We have been exploring what is old and new about the modern myth, and have seen the delicate balancing act that is creating such a work. However, this duality of new and old also exists for a final important theme in *The Sandman*: the art of storytelling. Of course, the act of telling stories is as old as the human race, but there is something new about the way that the modern storyteller is placed in the role of mythmaker. And if myths are gone, then what we have to replace them is stories. David Miller, in his discussion of the form of the next spiritual movement, remarked that the new theology would be a theology of stories and narrative (75), and this seems to be as good a guess as any. We have already examined various aspects of myth, and although we have alluded to it a few times, there remains one final step: for what are myths, if not stories? Myths are important stories, even central to our lives, or just, as I would suggest, the *big* stories. Still, if we are to believe the critics of modernity, then those of us who can claim to live with a story, to feel it in your bones (or as Delirium would say, in your socks), are the lucky few. You may remember from childhood a state somewhat similar to this, of being gripped by tales of fantastic and far-away worlds, or the inspired lunacy of a beloved children's writer. In this age of instant publishing, it seems that anyone can be an author, but only a few can truly be called "storytellers." For what is mythmaking, if not storytelling?

Campbell, who seems to have foreseen so much of Gaiman's work, was far from the first to note that the storytellers are the mythmakers of today, when he said that mythology is "the homeland of the muses," the motivating force behind literature and art (Power 55). And if the storytellers are "the new mythmakers," this arrangement is hardly new—good storytellers have always been held in high reverence. Put another way, the death of wonder, or of meaning, which people have referred to is in many ways a death of storytelling. Of course, nothing as central to human existence as storytelling could ever truly die, but we do have to ask the question: when was the last time a story held you in full aesthetic arrest, unable to think about anything else but to marvel at its composition and fluidity of movement, as it unfurled itself across the room?

The point of all this, of course, it that Gaiman is just such a storyteller. It has always been a truism of the writing world that writers love to write about nothing more than the process of writing. So it seems fitting that a master storyteller would have lots to say about the art of storytelling. And *Sandman* is filled with all facets of storytelling: people telling stories, writing stories, listening to stories, *living* stories. Frank McConnell, speaking of the story about stories (in his introduction to "The Kindly Ones") says "this is the kind of writing literary critics like to call 'postmodern:' letting the reader know you're conscious of what you're doing at the very time you do it. And a writer like Gaiman is smart enough to realize that kind of performance is about as 'modern' as the Divine Comedy. The great storytellers have always wanted to tell us as much about the business of storytelling as about the stories themselves" (4). And as we will see, *Sandman* also takes us into the mind of storytellers, both mundane (the doomed waitress Bettie in "24 Hours"), fanciful (the tricksterish faery Cluracan), and masterful (the Bard himself), for a "behind the scenes" look at the creative process. In a sense, *Sandman* is what might be called a "metanarrative," a story about stories. In addition, *Sandman* emerges as a hybrid text, with oral and written elements, in a blending of myth and folklore. More than that, Dream is, simply put, the reason we tell stories. Both oral and written storytelling are explored, and it seems that oral storytellers are somewhat privileged, at least in places. Still, both media are vital to the process of mythmaking. However, first we will examine the role of the artist in fashioning the modern myth. And just as we have an instinct for religion, so do we have one for storytelling. Stories are also capable of evoking Campbell's first (mystical) and fourth (psychological) functions of myth.

The strongest statements about the artist as mythmaker come, fittingly (because of his artistic temperament) from Campbell. In *The Power of Myth*, he writes "Myth must be kept alive. The people who can keep it alive are artists of one kind or another. The function of the artist is the mythologization of the environment and the world" (85). Later, Bill Moyers asks Campbell who are to be the shamans of today, and Campbell answers "It is the function of the artist to do this. The artist is the one who communicates myth for today. But he has to be an artist who understands mythology and humanity and isn't simply a sociologist with a program for you" (Power 99). It should be apparent by now that Gaiman has a firm grasp of the world's mythological traditions. And an understanding of human nature is critical to any artist's success. But Campbell's words hold another implication; if the artist is the one who creates the new mythology, then he or she holds a vital importance to the mind and soul of a society. In a sense, for those with the talent to do so, being an artist is *the highest good one can achieve*. Campbell speaks of mythology as "the secret opening through which the inexhaustible energies of the cosmos pour into human cultural manifestation" (Hero with a Thousand Faces 3). It is the role of the artist, then, to take this experience and translate it into a form that people can comprehend. In this sense, the artist and certain kinds of mystics have something in common: both experience something available to only a few and bring it back to the people as something they can understand.

It might also go without saying, but Campbell also lists myth as being behind the work of artists, even if they are not consciously seeking to create the new myth. He says that "mythology teaches you what's behind literature and the arts, it teaches you about your own life" (Power 11). He also states that

"I think of mythology as the homeland of the muses, the inspirers of art, the inspirers of poetry. To see life as a poem and yourself participating in a poem is what myth does for you" (Power 55). Campbell also lays out the connection of the artist to mythology as: "it's to see the experience and archetypology of a *living* moment. What the artist must render is a living moment somehow, a living moment actually in action or an inward experience" (Hero's Journey 184). One might take issue with Campbell's admittedly quite elastic definition of mythology, but the spirit of his remarks is important. One of the qualifications of a myth, then, is for a narrative to grip you, so that you see it as a part of your life, or see your life as a part of it. Campbell said that "When the story is in your mind, then you see its relevance to something happening in your own life. It gives you perspective on what's happening to you" (Power 4). Later, we will address some of the criticisms of Campbell, but for now it is enough to note that, at heart, he was more artist than academic. He had a reverence for the creative life that I have not found an equal to anywhere else. Elsewhere, he writes: "[the] personal creative act is related to the realm of myth, the realm of the muses, because myth is the homeland of the inspiration of the arts. The muses are the children of the goddess of memory, which is not the memory from up there, from the head; it is the memory of down here, from the heart" (Mythic 151).

So far we have encountered many descriptions of being gripped by a story; to this we would add "Proper art is static. It holds you in ecstatic arrest . . . Because the rhythm before you is the rhythm of nature. It is the rhythm of *your* nature . . . And why is it that you are held in aesthetic arrest? It is because the nature you are looking at is *your* nature. There is an accord between you and the object, and that is why you say, 'Aha!'" (Campbell, Mythic 154). Elsewhere, Campbell says, "that *Aha!* That you get when you see an artwork that really hits you is 'I am that.' I am the radiance and energy that is talking to me through this painting" (Hero's Journey 38). What we have seen, then, are various ways to describe a narrative's resonance with the reader (or listener). It may require a leap of faith to accept, but what is being argued for the magic of storytelling, and the transformative power of mythic narratives. As Bender says, "transforming lives is what stories are for" (178).

Like Campbell, Jung also recognizes the role of the artist in shaping myth. And he presents a corollary to Campbell, that the arts, mythology included, come from the psyche. He says that "the human psyche is the womb of all the sciences and arts" (Modern Man 152). Nancy Mellon adds that "a treasure-trove of imaginative powers lives within us all" (1). Jung also makes a distinction between psychological and visionary art. While psychological art involves the realm of human life, with the visionary, "the experience that furnishes the material for artistic expression is no longer familiar. It is a strange something that derives its existence from the hinterland of man's mind—that suggests the abyss of time separating us from pre-human ages, or evokes a super-human world of contrasting light and darkness. It is a primordial experience . . . It is a vision of other worlds" (Modern Man 156-7). For Jung, the "primordial experience" is essential, as "we must admit that the vision represents a deeper and more impressive experience than human passion . . . we cannot doubt that the vision is a genuine, primordial experience" (162). He also writes that "It is therefore to be expected of the poet that he will resort to mythology in order to give his experience its most fitting expression" (164). As strange and unusual as this sort of art may be, "it is not wholly unfamiliar. Man has known of it from time immemorial—here, there, and everywhere" (163). This kind of implicit knowledge and memory, then, is built into our very psyches.

Among psychologists, the term for such an art is "fantasy," which is also one of the genres into which *Sandman* is placed. Of course, as a genre, "fantasy" has garnered its share of critical disdain. However, to call it fantasy is not necessarily to deprecate it, as Jung tells us, "Truth to tell, I have a very high opinion of fantasy . . . When all is said and done, we are never proof against fantasy . . . All the works of man have their origin in creative fantasy. What right have we then to deprecate imagination? In the ordinary course of things, fantasy does not easily go astray; it is too deep for that, and too closely bound up with the tap-root of human and animal instinct" (Modern Man 66). He closes his statement by saying "As Schiller says, man is completely human only when he is playing" (66). Among psychologists, especially David Winnicott, playing, far from being a waste of time, is vital to establishing a person's relationships with others and the world. To identify fantasy with children, as many critics do, is really a backhanded slight (as being "childish" has become in our society a criticism) that reveals a deeper truth. For it is with children that we identify the feeling of wide-eyed wonder and mystery, the same kind of wonder that comprises Campbell's first function of mythology. Perhaps this is what Jesus meant when he said that in order to enter the kingdom of heaven, we must be like children (Matthew 18:3). Finally, as a caution, it is important to note that for Jung, the "primordial experience" is unconscious and inexpressible to the conscious mind, while for Campbell, the process of fashioning myth is a conscious act. And while I lean towards the latter view, Jung is helpful in recognizing a level deeper than consciousness at which a narrative can grip a person. And if the old mythic forms are gone, then the modern situation is that our storytellers must find a way to replace them. Put another way, we can only create myths if we dare to tell stories.

Having thus established the role of the artist in fashioning myth, and as our greatest hope for creating a distinctively modern myth, and having seen how a story can grip a person *below* the consciousness, we are ready to examine the role of stories and storytelling in *The Sandman*, with which the series is filled. And although Dream is the "Prince of Stories" (Sandman 2:3), and himself the reason we tell stories in the first place, it is often when the focus shifts away from Dream that the theme of storytelling moves to the forefront. At this point, Dream becomes a facilitator for the stories; we have already examined the relationship between myth and dreams, so it should seem fitting that the King of Dreams is also the Prince of Stories.

We have already alluded to the idea of claiming a story of one's own, and interpreting one's own life through that story. This is what it means to *live* a myth. In theology, there is a movement called "narrative theology" that proposes we do just this.

Speaking of narrative theology, George Stroup says that "every philosophical anthropology . . . must come to terms with the narrative structure of human identity" (87). Using the example of Christian narratives, he says that "to understand Christian narrative properly is to be able to interpret one's personal identity by means of biblical texts" (96). Next, he adds that "it is no accident that when they are asked to identify themselves most people recite a narrative or story" (Stroup 111). Furthermore, it soon becomes apparent that there is more to every person than meets the eye (111), a theme picked up on in Barbie's "secret worlds" speech. The more artistic side of these ideas is the fact that "if we experience the reality of each part of the story as an aspect of ourselves, no matter how grand or dilapidated, or fantastical it may be, it will be an enlivening experience" (Mellon 2). For us, the impact of these ideas is that stories and storytelling, of both the secular and sacred kind, are vital to our collective and individual identities. This is why I am spending so much time discussing the art of storytelling. Again and again, we see the importance of *living* a story.

While *The Sandman* contains examples of both oral and written stories, perhaps it would be advantageous to begin with written tales, since they are the closest to what Gaiman is doing, and since, after all, we live in a culture of the book. The key writers to appear in the series are Richard Madoc in "Calliope" (issue 17), the waitress Bettie from "24 Hours" (issue 6), the playwright in "Fear of Falling," . . . and an aspiring poet and playwright named William Shakespeare.

The story of the writer in "Fear of Falling" is perhaps the simplest of the accounts of storytellers. One reason for this is that it did not occur in a regular issue of *Sandman*, but in a publication of shorter stories by many of the artists on Gaiman's Vertigo label. Still, Gaiman saw fit to include it in one of the short story collections. It involves a playwright named Todd Faber, who is in the middle of directing a play he wrote. He is afraid, either of failure or of success, or of both, so he decides to abandon the production and run away. That night, he has a dream in which he is climbing up a cliff, and when he reaches the top, he encounters Dream, who questions him.

Todd answers "It's all getting to be too much for me. I feel I'm out of my depth. I'm scared. I'm scared I'm going to do something stupid" (Fables & Reflections 7). Dream answers, "And if you do something stupid, what then?" Todd says that he is afraid of falling, to which Dream replies, "It is sometimes a mistake to climb; it is always a mistake never even to make the attempt . . . If you do not climb you will not fall. This is true. But is it that bad to fail, that hard to fall? Sometimes you wake, and sometimes, yes, you die. But there is a third alternative" (7-8). At this point, Todd falls, and we do not find out what happens until the next morning, when he returns to the rehearsal, and says, "Sometimes you wake up. Sometimes the fall kills you. And sometimes, when you fall, you fly" (11). This story is the least complicated, and the most straightforwardly romantic, of the author narratives. It is addressed to anyone trying to find the courage to create, to take that great risk of putting oneself on the line and coming up with something no one has ever produced before. The falling, of course, is symbolic of a great many fears of failure. Everyone falls at one time or another, but sometimes, the result of the fall is that you learn how to fly. As Dream says, it may sometimes be a mistake to climb, but it is always a mistake not to try at all. If we are to continue to have myths in our world, then we must have men and women who are brave enough to risk failure and create them. Also, the story underscores the point that dreams, like myths, can be filled with wisdom and guidance.

The other narratives of writers involve, in one way or another, cautions about the dangers of writing. The second story (and the first chronologically) is of the waitress Bettie in "24 Hours." The narrator tells us that "On her days off, after she's tidied the house, Bette Munroe writes stories. She writes them in longhand on yellow legal pads. Sometimes she writes about her ex-husband Bernard, and about her son, Bernard Jr., who went off to college and never came back to her. She makes these stories end happily. Most of her stories, however, are about her customers" (Sandman 6:1). Although the stories might not be much as far as the craft goes, they add meaning to Bette's life, as "They look at her and they just see a waitress; they don't know she's nursing a secret. A secret that keeps her aching calf-muscles and her coffee-scalded fingers and her weariness from dragging her down . . . It's her secret. She's never shown anyone her stories" (6:1-2). Her dreams become all the more poignant as we begin to see through them. She dreams of sending her stories to a famous writer, who would publish them, of becoming famous, even being interviewed by Johnny Carson: "'But you're a writer,' Johnny Carson will say to her, 'How do you know what it's like to be a waitress?' She'll smile. She won't tell him. It'll be her secret" (6:2). She does not seem to realize that almost all writers start out working day jobs; however, the important thing for her is the dream. We have already seen how dreams can change the world, but for Bette, it is enough that her dream keep the monotony of working in a greasy spoon at bay. Gaiman also uses Bette to show the contrast between people's appearances, or the way we *want* to see them, and the harsh realities of life. In her stories, everyone gets a happy ending, as "All Bette's stories have happy endings. That's because she knows where to stop. She's realized the real problem with stories—if you keep them going long enough, they always end in death" (6:4). Besides almost tipping Gaiman's hand for what he has planned for the whole series, with the death of Dream, it shows her blind optimism, and what happens when you refuse to see reality.

"24 Hours" is also one of the truly horrific tales in *Sandman*; everyone ends up dead, either by his or her own hand or each other's, because of the machinations of John Dee and Dream's stolen ruby. Over the rest of the story, we find out the customers' stories. There is Judy, who just has a fight with her girlfriend, Donna (who later appears as Foxglove). Bette feels "sorry" for them, and in her stories marries them off to "fine young men" (6:3). She describes the Fletchers as "like lovebirds," but he dreams of having sex with a prostitute in his car and then beating her up, while she dreams of putting his head on a platter ("no more infidelities"). Marsh confesses that he "as good as killed" his wife by giving her, an alcoholic, a crate of vodka and going out of town for a week (6:18). Moreover, we learn that Bette's son ended up in prison after getting into prostitution. The whole story is shocking in its visceral nature, so it is somewhat difficult to know what to make of it all. But one thing is that Bette does not see the truth, and in her quest for happy endings, ignores reality. She is surely not a mythmaker, then; however, she does have the dream of being a writer, and for someone with her station in life, it is enough, until supernatural forces intervene. As an episode in the greater myth, "24 Hours" is also about the problem of evil, and the failure of moral and ethical systems to address it. For this slaughter has no meaning, no higher explanation of why God would allow such a thing to happen. It is as senseless as it is sudden, and there is no one to stop the madman with the ruby. Although Bette is flawed as a writer, she does not deserve what happens to her (neither do most of the rest of them), but such is often the way with cautionary tales, in which the protagonists come to a gruesome fate they did not deserve. After all, their story is also a plot device, in showing the twisted mind of John Dee when he takes hold of Dream's stolen ruby. A bad guy always needs victims.

Only slightly better off than Bette is Richard Madoc, the main character in "Calliope." The author of a successful first novel, he is nine months overdue on his second, and has been unable to write anything. As a result, he makes a deal with Erasmus Fry, an aging author, for his special "property:" the Muse Calliope who he had imprisoned years ago while in Greece. His treatment of her is horrific, as "His first action was to rape her, nervously, on the musty old camp bed. She's not even human, he told himself. She's thousands of years old. But her flesh was warm, and her breath was sweet, and she choked back tears like a child whenever he hurt her. It occurred to him momentarily that the old man might have cheated him: given him a real girl. That he, Rick Madoc, might possibly have done something wrong, even criminal" (Sandman 17:8). The irony compounds as the tale continues, as Madoc becomes wildly successful. He keeps Calliope until Dream shows up and gives him an excess of ideas that overwhelm him (reminiscent of the "ironic punishment" division of the Greek Hades), until he lets her go. The tale might also work as a way for Gaiman to assuage his conscience as a writer, as it may seem that all authors are "raping the muse," figuratively if not literally. Thus, it may have been a Gaiman-style autobiography. At a party, Madoc is praised for transcending the bounds of genre fiction—enough to be nominated for a mainstream literary award. Gaiman won the World Fantasy Award for the "Midsummer Night's Dream" story—making it the first and only time a comic has won a mainstream award. In the same panel, a female fan praises him for the strong women in his work, to which he responds "Actually, I do tend to regard myself as a feminist writer" (17:12). I do not know if Gaiman has made any such claim himself, but his work has been praised by many as containing strong female characters. The tale ends when Madoc lets Calliope go, and he says "it's gone. I've got no idea any more. No idea at all" (17:24). Even if Madoc is not some kind of twisted alter-ego of the writer, it reveals what some people will do to avoid or get rid of writer's block. On theme here, that we have seen elsewhere, is that people are capable of committing terrible wrongs, and that we should try to reduce people's suffering whenever we can. With Madoc, the problem is not that he is a monster, but that he is very human; as he does something terrible, he is a reminder of the evil that exists around and especially within us.

From "24 Hours" and "Calliope," one might think that the outlook for writers is rather bleak. Either they blind themselves to reality and use their dreams to stave off the boredom of a meaningless life, or they will resort to terrible measures in order to ensure that the ideas keep coming. Compared to them, then, the outlook for William Shakespeare is positively rosy. Still, even though Shakespeare makes his deal to become the greatest storyteller of his age (and some would say of any age), in the end, he comes to half-regret his choice. Will's story begins when he and Marlowe are eating in the same inn where Dream meets Hob for their once-a-century drink. At this point, Shakespeare is a hack, who Marlowe encourages to give up writing, and who wants more than anything to become a great writer. He tells Marlowe that "I would give anything to have your gifts. Or more than anything to give men dreams, that would live on long after I am dead. I'd bargain, like your Faustus, for that boon" (Sandman 13:12). Dream overhears the conversation and asks Will, "Would you write great plays? Create new dreams to spur the minds of men?" (13:13). They go off and talk, and although we do not see their exchange, we know that Dream unlocks the doors in Will's mind, to allow him to become a vehicle of the great stories. Will, in exchange, promises to write two plays for Morpheus, celebrating dreams, which turn out to be *A Midsummer Night's Dream* and *The Tempest*.

The story of "Midsummer" is told in issue 19, as Shakespeare's players perform in front of an audience of faery folk, including Titania and Auberon (the queen and king of Faerie). By this time, we can see the seeds of discontent, even in the face of Will's greatness. His son, Hamnet, traveling with him for the Summer, says "He's very distant...Anything that happens he just makes stories out of it. I'm less real to him than any of the characters in his plays" (Sandman 19:13). He says that his sister Judith jokes that if he died, Will would just write a play about it... "Hamnet." (Of course, just this happens.) Hamnet ends the exchange by saying "All that matters to him...All that matters is the stories" (19:13). Even Dream begins to wonder if he did the right thing, as he is beginning to ponder his role and influence in people's lives. He tells Titania, "I wonder, Titania. I wonder if I have done right. And I wonder why I wonder. Will is a willing vehicle for the great stories. Through him they will live for an age of man; and his words will echo down through time. But he did not understand the price. Mortals never do. They only see the prize, their heart's desire, their dream...But the price of getting what you want, is getting what you once wanted" (19:19). This statement seems pessimistic, that even if you get what you want, you won't be happy because you won't be the same person who wanted it. But, fundamentally, it amounts to another affirmation of change, the radical change that can go on inside each one of us, that we must accept as part of our lives.

Shakespeare's story continues in the final *Sandman* (issue 75), which takes place as he is writing his second play for Dream, *The Tempest*, which also happened to be the last play he wrote alone. This time, an older Shakespeare is actively questioning the deal he made with Dream. He talks to a priest, asking how to redeem the magician Prospero, but of course he is also asking about himself. When he meets Dream, he asks him what his life would have been like, had he not made their deal, but then he shrinks away when Dream starts to tell him (Sandman 75:179). He says, "I wonder . . . I wonder if it was all worth it. Whatever happened to me in life, happened to me as a writer of plays. I'd fall in love, or fall in lust. And at the height of my passion, I would think, 'So this is how it feels,' and I would tie it up with pretty words. I watched my life as if it were happening to someone else. My son died. And I was hurt; but I watched my hurt, and even relished it, a little, for now I could write a real death, a true loss" (75:180). Again, here it seems that Gaiman is trying to tell the reader about the mind of the writer, and the terrible price it exacts on those who follow the craft. My brother, who is much more of a writer than I will ever be, tells me that the feeling of watching your own life with detachment, as a way of gathering material, is quite true. Dream reveals to Will that even if he did open the door in the playwright's mind, it was Will who still did the writing, and all the work. Will then asks Dream why he chose *The Tempest*, and Dream (in one of the series' most heartbreaking moments) tells him that he "wanted a play about graceful ends . . . about a King who drowns his books, and breaks his staff, and leaves his kingdom. About a magician who becomes a man. About a man who turns his back on magic" (75:181). When asks why, Dream continues, "Because I will never leave my island," and later, "I am not a man. And I do not change. I asked you earlier if you saw yourself reflected in your tale. I do not. I may not. I am prince of stories, Will; but I have no story of my own. Nor shall I ever" (75:182). The tale (Gaiman's, that is) also tells about the terrible price of writing by examining the life of one of the great storytellers of any age. Frank McConnell writes that the choice of Shakespeare is especially fitting, as "in [the Renaissance], our myths began to be humanized; beginning, say, with Shakespeare, we began to realize that the gods had not invented us, but that we were in the process of inventing our gods" ("Epic Comics"). Thus, Shakespeare makes an ideal study for Gaiman's purposes, to say nothing of the artistic nerve necessary to take on the Bard, with which fortunately for us, Gaiman is quite blessed. Incidentally, it is worth noting that Gaiman chose

Shakespeare's story as the final issue of the series. Thus, the last we see of Dream is (the old Dream) lamenting his lack of story (which is, of course, pure irony: we are reading his story). From this, I believe we can infer that for Gaiman, the storytelling material is an essential part of the series as a whole.

Overall, the depictions of writers depict the terrible price the craft exacts: from them, and from those close to them. How are we to reconcile this with the idea of the storyteller as mythmaker? The answer, I believe, lies in the instances of oral storytelling that appear in *Sandman*. In a sense, there is something pure about oral narratives, and about people who view storytelling as an *art*, as opposed to writers, who view it as a *profession*. And while myths can be oral, more often the oral narratives are folklore, *the stories people tell each other*. There are even more examples of told stories in *Sandman* than written ones: the travelers in "World's End," the grandfather in "Tales in the Sand," Gilbert in "The Doll's House," and the storytellers of "Convergence" (issues 38-40). The best example of this is in "World's End," in which travelers from different worlds are trapped by a storm (a reality storm) in an inn and pass the time by telling tales. The frame of the story, of course, goes back to Chaucer's *Canterbury Tales*. On this choice of models, Gaiman remarks, "I liked the idea of using one of the oldest storytelling devices in the English language. If you're going to steal, you might as well do so from a great source, and *Canterbury Tales* definitely qualifies" (Bender 176).

The storytellers come from a variety of worlds and races: there are Brant and Charlene, whose car crashes on the way to Chicago, the centaur Chiron, the blue-skinned apprentice mortician Petrefax, the English sailor girl-passing-for-boy Jim, and the wily faerie Cluracan. Chaucer's story used characters from all different walks of life; Gaiman does him one better by bringing together characters *literally* from different worlds. And as seems to be the instinct, when we find ourselves among strangers for an extended period of time, we tell stories. Another notable feature of "World's End" is the nesting of stories within stories. In "Cerements," we have Petrefax telling his stories of life as an apprentice in the great Necropolis Litharge. He tells of attending a burial in which the participants all told stories. One of these tellers tells a story about meeting a traveler (Destruction) who was passing through the city. And the stranger tells his listener the story of the first Necropolis, and how its charter was revoked when its inhabitants became hardened and no longer loved their duties and recognized the importance of the funeral rites. And, at the end of the collection, we find that the whole thing has been a story, of Brant Tucker, our narrator, talking to a bartender. So we have a story, within a story, within a story . . . within another story. The frame story is a common story device, but to the best of my knowledge no one else has matched this depth of recursion.

Either way, the recursion certainly boggles the mind. Another thing to notice about "World's End" is the economy with which Gaiman works with elements of the larger tale. In "Cerements," we learn that one of the Endless has died in the past (the first Despair), and we see the room that holds the materials and the ritual to accompany the death of one of the Endless. Of course, this foreshadows Dream's demise, and the envoy Eblis O'Shaunnesey's (named by Delirium, if you can tell) seeking out the proper materials. Another foreshadowing event takes place in the last issue of the collection, as we see the funeral train going across the sky. We have already discussed this scene at some length; suffice it to say that it makes it clear that mourning is going to be a theme for a while. Overall, the storytelling, both in scope, levels, and humanity (as these are some of the finest examples of stories told for stories' sake), is (not to use a word too much) magical. It transforms the experience of everyone listening, and, just as Bender says, changes lives. After hearing all the stories, Brant's image of the world is shaken, Charlene decides to stay at the inn, and Petrefax decides to seek adventure outside the Necropolis. It is also worth noting that in most of these stories, Dream shows up rarely, if at all. It is as if Gaiman decided to put off the main plot for a while and focus for a while on storytelling, which is another thing that *The Sandman* is about.

In keeping with the theme, there are other accounts of oral storytelling in *Sandman*, and they all seem to focus on bringing people of different worlds together. The one that rises to mythic quality comes in "Tales in the Sand," the prelude to "The Doll's House." Here, we see a telling of the foundation myth of an African people, which is also a rite of passage. One of Eliade's criteria for sacred myths is that they are told only at certain times. This story is heard only once in a man's life, when he is initiated, and told only once, when he goes to initiate a relative of his. The story, which tells of Dream's disastrous affair with Nada (minus the condemning her to Hell part), also contains many elements of folklore and myth. In a sense, then, *The Sandman* is a hybrid text. The people are held to be the first people on earth, as "the first people were of our tribe. That is our secret, and we never tell outsiders, for they would kill us if they knew. But it is the truth" (Sandman 9:5). Campbell and others have noticed that just about every group has some myth in which they were "the first people." Gaiman's attention to detail is key here; the tale also features animals in important roles and other folkloristic devices. It is the little weaverbird that finds the fruit that will allow Nada to find Dream. However, the trip carrying the burning berry burns it, causing its color to change from white to brown. Also, a prohibition is set against killing the weaverbird, because of its service. All these are standard folkloristic elements. Finally, there is mention made of another version of the tale, in the stories that the women tell, "in their private language that the men-children are not taught, and that the old men are too wise to learn" (9:24). Here and in a few other places, a distinction is made between male and female stories, and it would make an interesting project to examine the gendering of stories as a greater theme in *Sandman*. (Gaiman has made some interesting comments about the "genders" of his stories as well.)

Also, with Nada's tale, we see an intact culture, with a living mythology. The uncle telling the story to his nephew shows that his people's religion and rites of passage sustain them in the way that, according to the critics of modernity, modern religion no longer does. If nothing else, this story serves as a reminder that, no matter how much we enjoy stories today, there was a time when people believed in stories completely, and it sustained them. The challenge for the modern myth, then, is to sustain us as traditional myths once did.

Finally, there are other instances of storytelling in *Sandman*, with the underlying theme, that stories bring people together. First, there is the mini-story-arc titled "Convergence" (issues 38-40), which features stories being told between generations and across worlds. In "The Hunt," a grandfather (who is secretly also a werewolf) tells his somewhat unwilling granddaughter about his adventures as a young man. On the theme of Gaiman's self-consciousness, at one point the granddaughter says "It all sounds suspiciously post-modern to me, Grandpa. Are you sure this is really a story from the old country?" (Sandman 38:11). In "Soft Places," a young Marco Polo meets a friend of his from later in life, and Gilbert, who is trying to get away from Dream and his new love (Thessaly). This story also introduces the idea that there are "soft places," where the fabric of space and time and reality grows thin and people can encounter others from other worlds and times. In "A Parliament of Rooks" (issue 40), Eve and Cain and Abel set about entertaining a pre-transfiguration Daniel. Eve tells the story of the three wives of Adam, Abel the story of how he and Cain came to live in the Dreaming (with the cutest Li'l Endless you ever saw). Cain, for his part, sets out a mystery about the behavior of rooks (a type of bird in the same family of ravens). Their plural is called a parliament, because of a strange behavior. They gather in a field in a circle, with one bird in the middle. That bird then begins to chatter for a time, until the group of birds either flies away or pecks the one in the middle to death. At the end of the issue, Abel tells Matthew and Daniel that the rook in the middle is really telling a story, and that the other birds either approve of the story (and fly away), or disapprove (and peck it to death). Thus, if we are to believe Gaiman, even animals have an instinct for storytelling. Again, as with much myth or folklore, a narrative occurs as a conversation between two or more people, including gods or archetypes. There are other instances of storytelling in the series, Gilbert telling Rose the original "Little Red Riding Hood" story, or the cat in "Dream of a Thousand Cats" telling her story, or the interlude of the old women telling Rose the story in the nursing home, but the point is clear: storytelling is the act that brings us all together, and is a part of why we have myths in the first place.

The amount and space and attention Gaiman devotes to storytelling is clear: what remains is to establish *why* he does so. And here, I can offer some suggestions why. In terms of the modern myth, we have already seen from Miller that the new theology would be a theology of stories. And *Sandman* is, in many ways, a story about stories. There are too many instances of story-telling, both oral and written, for us to ignore them. Of course, for metanarratives (stories about stories) we can go all the way back to *The Odyssey*. And the reason the great storytellers have always told us about the business of telling stories (besides a sense of their own importance) is their tremendous importance for the vitality of a culture. What we can get from Jung is that we might even be able to say that we have an *instinct* for storytelling. Nancy Mellon puts it that "there is a natural storytelling urge and ability in all human beings" (172). And if myths are really about the human condition, then one important aspect of myth should focus on *why* we tell myths in the first place. It seems to me that myths are an attempt to come to terms with the world we find around us. In our limited understanding, we create. Of course, we know more about the world than we did 3000 years ago, but in the things that really matter: our minds, our souls, our spirits, we still have much to learn. The point here is that *Sandman* is not only a story about stories: Dream, as the prefect of Dreaming and tales, is the reason we tell stories . . . and create myths. As Dream tells Titania of Faerie at one point, "Tales and dreams are the shadow-truths that will endure when mere facts are dust and ashes, and forgot" (Sandman 19:21).

Finally, there is another example of the creative life we have yet to mention: Destruction. Since he abandoned his realm, he has traveled far and wide, but eventually came to rest on a small island. There, he engages actively in creative pursuits: he paints, composes poems, cooks, and sculpts. It is not that he is a master craftsman; in fact, if we are to believe Barnabas, he is uniformly terrible at these tasks. But the important thing is that he finds happiness and meaning in the creative life as an artist, albeit a mediocre one.

Yet, if we pay attention to *Sandman*, then another important feature of myths is that they are, at bottom, stories. Here, we come to an important step in the definition of myth. How are myths different from stories? How are they related? In traditional societies, they seem intimately connected, as stories about people also involved divine beings, and stories about divine beings also involved people. In modern society, however, he have had a clearer line of demarcation. We have myths (which we call "religion") of our own culture on one level, then stories (which we call "literature") and other people's myths on another level. Folklore, if given a place, would lie somewhere between myths and stories. Finally, there is a firm line between literature—high culture, and low culture, which includes "comic books." What *Sandman* should make clear is that the line between high and low culture is a false distinction. Here, in comics, we have a story that has all the meaning, all the grace, and all the subtlety, if not more, of "high-culture" literature. And if this distinction is false, then maybe the line between stories and myths is too. We have already seen "postmodern" writers taking on elements of the mythic in literature, and of course, literature is filled with mythic elements. Perhaps, then, what we are left with are *stories*. Myths, after all, have always been stories—what I have called the BIG stories, which ask the big questions of life. Who are we? Why are we here? Who made the world? Why do we die? And so on. Is it not possible that the difference between myths and stories is simply one of quality? That myths are simply well-told stories?

Of course, this criteria opens up the question of what makes a story well-told. Part of it is the emotional appeal, which we will discuss soon. The story must be good enough to become beloved, to reach the point where people order their lives according to it. And here, the criteria seems to be a depth of humanity that we find by feeling rather than reason. For emotional involvement with the characters is the beginning of living your life through a story. The key action here is to read (or hear) a story and see yourself reflected in it. In time, such a story can even provide identity, as myth once did for people. Part of the criteria should be subtlety, something that can be read and reread, and can reveal something new each time. Depending on the book, I have read through *Sandman* 6 or 7 times, and I have found something new in the stories every time. Finally, there is something hard to define, but I will call "command of the devices of storytelling." Simply put, Gaiman is a master storyteller: he knows how stories work, how people read them, how to lead a reader, and how to make the story curve at the last minute for maximum effect. Finally, a good story, if it is to rise to the level of myth, should fulfill Campbell's four functions of myth. First, *Sandman* is full of wonder, both overt and subtle. Second, it tells us about the structure of the macrocosm, what the universe is like and who rules it. Third, it provides a sociology, telling us how to be good, or *human*, to each other. Finally, fourth, it tells us how to move through the stages of our lives, from birth to the various rites of passage of puberty, marriage, and old age, and finally, death (the BIG change). The point here is that stories and storytelling bring people together. It is for all these reasons that *Sandman* is a good story. And more important, why it is a myth.

The art of storytelling is, of course, older than anyone can remember. However, it also contains the paradox of the modern myth of being both old and new. Whoever created the original myths, their torch has been passed to the storytellers of today, secular as well as religious. Just like the high-culture / low-culture divide has been broken down, so has that which formerly separated stories from myths proper. We previously spent some time lamenting the loss of meaning and religion in the modern world. And while it is certainly true that the old traditions no longer sustain many of us, we must also not be swept away by pessimism; rather, we must look at what has emerged to take their place. The purpose of the discussion of the role of the art of storytelling in *The Sandman* has been to emphasize that storytelling is not dead. And just as the mythmakers helped sustain the life of their communities in ancient times, so do the storytellers of today. If one is willing to look, there are many storytellers who incorporate the mythic into their works (Charles de Lint, Garth Ennis, Joss Whedon, to name a few). Furthermore, it is not just on their shoulders that we place the weighty task of creating meaning; the "collective unconscious" and the example of Destruction tell us that we all have it in us to be creative beings. The old ways are gone, just like Dream's Ruby was destroyed by John Dee. And like Dream, we cannot go back to the way it once was. However, the positive side of this is that all the energies we put into them have been freed for our use. So it is that in the modern world, we make our own meanings. *And we're doing fine.*

CONCLUSION: HANGIN' OUT
WITH THE DREAM KING

"... seems I keep getting the story twisted, so where's Neil when you need him?"

—Tori Amos

Looking back, we have covered a lot of ground in trying to establish *Sandman* as a modern myth. We have examined the relationship between myth and dream. And while there are important differences between the two, there is also a definite kinship, on both a personal and societal level. Gaiman (consciously or not) picks up on this kinship, by setting the series in dreams, and establishing Dream, the embodiment of dream, as the central character. Also, Gaiman's "Dreaming" is intimately related to Jung's idea of the collective unconscious.

We have encountered perhaps the most famous and prevalent myth—the hero's journey—and examined the ways the central plot of *Sandman*, Dream's process of becoming human, is a kind of hero myth, with new implications for the classic model. Also, we have found heroism on the part of many of the series' supporting characters, especially in their relationships with other people—one of the things that makes us human.

We have opened a dialogue with Becker, who posited that all of human endeavors are aimed at allaying the central fear of human existence: the fear of death—certainly a modern myth would have to address this as well. With this in mind, we have traced the role of death in the series, both as a condition, and in its personification as Death, Dream's cutie-pie older sister. Also, we have watched the process of mourning the dead, especially Dream, in the series.

We have examined the religious concepts of freedom and responsibility in the series, and have seen how, in the end, rules and responsibilities can become the subtlest of traps, or an excuse to keep us from doing what we truly have to do. And although it may not be the ultimate freedom, we always have the option to walk away, or to do what truly must be done.

We have seen how *Sandman* serves, not to validate a given social order as Campbell suggests, but to criticize and try to change aspects of the present social order that are too restrictive for modern life. In this way, myth becomes a vehicle for social change. We have also encountered Miller, who believes that the answer to our spiritual dilemma is a new polytheism, and from there we have moved to an examination of new and old elements that compromise *Sandman*, elements that seem essential to the idea of the modern myth.

Finally, we have seen the role of the artist as mythmaker. Campbell and Jung agree that the key to finding new spiritual fulfillment lies in the individual artists. We have also found another way of looking at myth: as stories. The art of storytelling, then, is central, and we have seen the multitude of characters in *Sandman* who are involved in telling stories. The storytellers also lead us to the realization that, at their heart, myths are stories: the really important stories. What we need, then, are storytellers.

Thus, we have accounted for the bulk of the discussion that has transpired here. However, there remain a few points to make before the discussion concludes. The first involves the sources we have used. Joseph Campbell has been with us throughout the journey, so his work deserves some comment. First, I must admit that in using his discussions of myth, I have stretched his words to some extent. When he spoke of myths as society's dreams, or gods as magnified dreams, he was of course being metaphorical (as there is no literal process by which a dream is turned into a god, for example). However, in Gaiman, these concepts are used literally, and fundamentally we are dealing with two different levels of reality. However, I think Campbell would approve. Gaiman once said that the main business of fantasy is to make metaphors concrete (Notes from the Underground). From what we have seen, it really does look as if Gaiman had some of Campbell's passages in mind when he set out to create the universe of *Sandman*. Overall, one of the things I get from the series is a respect for and love of myth. Gaiman says that "I love religion and I love myth. People say 'Why?' and the only answer I can give is because I'm me." This enthusiasm for myth seems at this point unparalleled . . . except in Campbell.

Which brings us to the second and final point about Campbell: criticisms of his work. In academic circles, many people have criticized Campbell for overstating similarities, confounding categories, and making grand generalizations. In his study of Campbell's work, Robert Segal says "One the one hand, then, Campbell is the grandest defender of myth. On the other hand he is oddly not much interested in myth—as myth. He is much more interested in human nature, which he simply finds revealed in myths . . . He is far more concerned with the information myths contain than the myths themselves" (137). To some degree, I think these things are true. Campbell himself admits that the greatest effect his students had on his writing was that rather than just looking at the myths in themselves, they forced him to find out how the myth related to their lives. He also refers to the field of mythology as "a very large academic field of facts, facts, facts, all over the place," but that his students were more interested in *life* (Hero's Journey 60, 91). Returning to Segal, he sums up his criticisms of Campbell when he says that "these criticisms pale beside the prime one: that Campbell spends too much time reveling in myth and not enough time analyzing it" (140). To this, I would answer: "What is wrong with that?" I agree that Campbell's accounts of myths are not as exhaustive as some other scholars', and that he makes some hard and fast statements about traditions that are really much more complicated than that. He is also too socially conservative, and does not acknolwedge the ways in which myth can critique a social order. However, in my mind he more than makes up for of his shortcomings with his enthusiasm. Campbell's writings are so interesting in part because it is apparent that he is actually *enjoying* what he is doing. It is no wonder, then, that Campbell has found a warmer reception in the populace than among academics. To me, it goes back to his first function of myth: mystical wonder is not a very "good" place from which to produce serious scholarly writing, but what a state to be in! The truth of the matter is: Campbell was never an academic. He lived in academia, but all the time he was secretly an artist.

When Campbell died in 1987, *The Sandman* was just starting to get off the ground. It may have been intentional, then, that one of the victims of John Dee's chaos is named "Joey Campbell"—a nod to the scholar? Either way, I feel that Campbell would have loved Gaiman's work, and would have devoted much time and attention to reading and studying it. (After all, *Sandman* is much more complex and sophisticated than the "Star Wars" movies that Campbell raved about.) Indeed, many parts of *Sandman* seem to have been written with Campbell in mind. The Summer I discovered *Sandman*, I also read *The Power of Myth* for the first time. Together, they ended up rekindling in me a long-time love of myth and story. In a way, this project is meant as a tribute to Campbell . . . I am writing about *Sandman* because he never got to. Campbell is the *reason* one can now express an interest in studying mythology without just getting blank looks in return. He also taught me that a life of study need not be a kind of slow, suffocating death. Campbell also speaks of "following your bliss," which is whatever excites and fulfills you, as "if you do follow your bliss you put yourself on a kind of track that has been there all the while, waiting for you, and the life you ought to be living is the one you are living . . . I say, follow your bliss and don't be afraid, and doors will open where you didn't know they were going to be" (Power 120) What is clear to me is that Campbell was a person who followed his bliss, and it took him far. And the idea of following one's bliss, more than anything else, is why I am writing this.

It is time, then, to wrap up the bulk of this discussion by returning to where we started: the modern sense of alienation and loneliness that pervades a world of reason, without gods, without myth. One of the points I have tried to argue is that the truth of the matter is not so simple. As even Eliade admits, the instinct for the sacred is still alive and well; one just has to know where to look for it. Just because it is hard to envision a fully functioning modern myth does not mean that it is impossible to have one. We have encountered the idea before of living with a story, and making it part of you, so that it surrounds and pervades your life. Jung tells us of a time when he discovered that "hardly had I finished the manuscript when it struck me what it means to live with a myth, and what it means to live without one . . . Hence the man who thinks he can live without myth, or outside it, is an exception. He is like one uprooted, having no true link either with the past, or with the ancestral life which continues within him, or yet with contemporary society" (quoted in Campbell, Intro to *The Portable Jung*, xxi). The importance of living a myth, simply put, cannot be overstated. Campbell tells us that Jung once asked himself "what myth are you living?" He found that he did not know, so he set out to discover it (Intro to *The Portable Jung*, xxi). I have been living with *Sandman* for five years now. (I came to the series late; many fans have been there since the beginning ten years ago.) And in order to explain its effects, we must expand our discussion a little.

It is true that, to this point, I have been engaged primarily in an intellectual discussion. But the reasons we need myth, and the place of myth in our lives, have all been examinations of emotional issues. To talk about the fear of death is useless without the experience of one's own sometimes paralyzing fear that one day we will simply cease to be. We cannot identify with a hero-figure unless we are able to place oneself inside that figure and feel what he or she feels. Likewise, the spiritual problem of modernity makes little sense unless one can actually feel the ache of a loss of meaning. In the end, what makes *Sandman* so compelling is its emotional appeal. To address this side of the series, I have solicited input from other fans of the series about what drew them to Gaiman's work. One fan says, "I put myself inside of those books and cuddled with the characters. When they felt emotions, so did I: Sandman took dives into the realm of dreams and feelings it made me feel that I could do more with my life. Every single one of those books found that heart in me. . . . Life wasn't a confusion anymore" (personal communication). Another fan adds that "Suddenly the thoughts I had about life, the ones I had not been able to express, had names. I had words to explain how my heart, and the hearts of people around me worked . . . It was more effective than therapy, or any anti-anxiety drugs they'd thrown my way. And there was enormous comfort discovering that yes, I was not alone in the damned world, someone out there did think like me." A third fan put it that "The themes in the stories are something that parallel actual life, whether of not the particulars are the same . . . You might not be Rose Walker, moving around nearly ageless, but you know the feeling that you don't quite belong, that you're not quite like everyone else, that there's something missing inside of you that keeps you from being normal no matter how hard you try . . . You know these characters as people, even if they're not, because they *feel* real. They carry with them the weight of emotions that pull at you and draw you in close. You can almost feel them in your friends, in yourself, in people you know and see all around you." Other fans echoed themes that we have already examined. One says that "it gave me a sense of the mysterious (mystical, even) hiding behind the mundane," bringing up memories of Campbell's "invisible plane of support" or Eliade's sacred space and time existing behind the profane. Finally, another reader wrote "They speak to me on a bonedeep level, just like racial myths/memories. In fact, when I first read them it seemed to me he was *writing* myths, his stories resonate on that level. He's a Storyteller with a capital S, and a very big part of who we are is that we listen to stories . . . stories create us and give us identity and life beyond the everyday . . . stories are so important to everyone, they're food for the soul." I couldn't have put it better myself.

However, it would be unfair of me to come this far, and use others' words about *The Sandman*'s emotional impact without telling my story. I experienced a severe depression towards the end of high school, which I came out of the Summer before I started college. But after about a month of school, I experienced a second episode, much worse than the first, and I came home after the first semester, with no idea what I was going to do. For a few months, the music of Tori Amos literally kept me alive. Tori and Neil Gaiman are very good friends, and often make references to each other's work. (Some of Tori Amos's songs contain lines like "it you need me, me and Neil'll be hangin' out with the Dream King," and "seems I keep getting the story twisted so where's Neil when you need him?" Gaiman returns the favor by having Tori's "Tear in Your Hand" play in the bar at the beginning of "Brief Lives," and by calling Rose Walker a "cornflakes girl" [sic], after Amos's song "Cornflake Girl." Tori's music incidentally makes a wonderful soundtrack to reading *Sandman*.) One day in the bookstore, my brother picked up a graphic novel by "that comic guy Tori's always talking about," the first volume of *Sandman*. Two weeks later, I had the full set of ten volumes, and was reading them constantly, first as individual books, then as a whole series straight through. I can remember one night, reading through an issue and feeling this strange feeling welling up inside me, and realizing that, for the first time I could remember, *I wanted to live*. Putting it simply, *Sandman* helped me put my life back together. Finally, I need more than anyting to believe that there is more to life than what we see, that there is magic in the world. As Jill Sobule says, "I'd love to see a miracle once before I die. *Sandman* provides that, and tells us to always believe in miracles.

As far as passages, a few stand out as my favorites. One character we have not seen previously is Sexton Furnival, the main character in the first Death miniseries, *The High Cost of Living*. At the beginning of the story, the sixteen-year old wants to kill himself because his life holds no meaning. However, after spending the day with Death (on her once-a-century day as a mortal), he changes his mind, and gains a new perspective on life, and so may be a prototype for modern life. Another moment I love is in Rose Walker's journal at the end of "The Doll's House," when, after spending six months hiding out in her room, she emerges, saying "You can't feel cheated forever." One of the important themes in *Sandman* is what Campbell called "an affirmation of life," with all its pain and difficulty. Rose has had the foundations of her world shaken, but still she emerges. Also on this theme is Matthew at the end of "The Wake," accepting the new Dream, and saying "Funeral's over. Time to get on with our lives. Time to grow up." In a sense, the funeral was the past five years. These words helped me find the strength to get on with my life. And on the subject of "The Wake," I can attest to its function as a myth. I mourned Dream. I really did. And sometimes, I'm still overcome with sadness at his death. But I have to realize it was for the best. To illustrate: in the middle of the Summer I got into *Sandman*, my grandmother died. She hadn't been terribly ill, but she wasn't doing very well, either. But whenever I bring up her death to my mother, she always says, "but she was so tired." Likewise, right before Morpheus dies, he says to Death "I am tired, my sister. I am very tired" (Sandman 69:2). And just as *Sandman* helped me make sense of the loss of my grandmother, this phrase stuck with me, and made me think that sometimes, death can be a good thing, a release, no matter how much we fear it, or how much we miss those who we have lost.

However, my absolute favorite part comes at the end of "A Game of You." Before Barbie writes on Wanda's tombstone with the lipstick, she says "It's like, that people . . . Well, that everyone has a secret world inside of them. I mean everybody. All of the people in the whole world—no matter how dull and boring they are on the outside. Inside them they've all got unimaginable, magnificent, wonderful, stupid, amazing worlds . . . Not just one world. Hundreds of them. Thousands, maybe. Isn't that a weird thought?" (Sandman 37:19). I have always been extremely shy and quiet, and feel like because of that, I often come off as boring. But after reading Barbie's speech, I realize that even if I don't say anything, it's still okay, because I'm not just the quiet person standing in the corner; there's more than that to me—I've got secret worlds inside me. To me, this idea seems to be the basis of fantasy . . . and of myth. Inside everyone, there are unrecognized pantheons of gods, and worlds of untold wonders. And there is something about this story, this *myth*, that serves to bring them out in people, whether the worlds of myth are literal (Gaiman), metaphorical (Campbell), or biological (Jung).

In the end, it is the emotional impact of these stories that imparts the quality of myth. I have read other reconstructions of myth, and many of them seem to possess a definite cleverness. However, they often leave me cold. On the other hand, the stories in *Sandman* (and stories about stories, and stories about stories about stories . . .) are filled with warmth, humor, and (not to overuse the word) humanity. I love every one of these stories, and the characters are like old friends: brooding, alienated Dream, poor shattered Delirium, happy and practical Death, lovelorn Nuala, arrogant Hob Gadling, and Matthew,

Lucien, Destruction, Barnabas, Rose, Raine, Wanda, Barbie, Hazel & Foxglove, and a host of others. More importantly, I have *been* all these characters. It is this central humanity that makes *Sandman* so special. Put another way, these are *my* sacred texts; just thinking about some moments in the series makes me go teary.

One final quotation comes from issue 4, when Dream goes to Hell to regain his stolen helmet. He ends up challenging the demon Chronozon, and playing a shapeshifting game, in which the combatants take on different forms in order to defeat each other. The combat escalates, until Chronozon says "I am anti-life, the beast of judgement. I am the dark at the end of everything. The end of universes, gods, worlds . . . of everything" (Sandman 4:19). Dream responds, "I am hope." Of course, Chronozon cannot come up with anything to top that, and so he loses their game, for nothing can conquer hope. This is the greatest lesson of *The Sandman*, that no matter what happens, hope will continue to exist. In her introduction to the first Death mini-series, Tori Amos ends a delightfully loopy meditation on Death with "and after all she has a brother who believes in hope." Through death, hardship, and pain, there is hope. And in the modern world, what we need most of all, what people seem to have lost, is hope. And hope is what will lead us back to meaning, and to joy. Peter Straub ends his afterword to "Brief Lives" by saying, "If this isn't literature, nothing is" (6). I would add: if this isn't myth, then nothing is. For if the way has been "lost" in the modern world, then the final legacy of *The Sandman* may be the reclamation of our emotions in an "emotionless" age, by simultaneously addressing the heart, mind, and soul. Indeed, no greater comment or praise could be made about a myth in any age.

BIBLIOGRAPHY

PRIMARY SOURCES:

Gaiman, Neil. *Death: The High Cost of Living*. New York: DC Comics, 1994.

—*Death: The Time of Your Life*. New York: DC Comics, 1997.

—"Murder Mysteries." *Angels and Visitations*. Minneapolis: DreamHaven Books, 1993, 139-166.

—*The Sandman: Brief Lives*. New York: DC Comics, 1994

—*The Sandman: The Doll's House*. New York: DC Comics, 1990.

—*The Sandman: Dream Country*. New York: DC Comics, 1990.

—*The Sandman: Fables and Reflections*. New York: DC Comics, 1993.

—*The Sandman: A Game of You*. New York: DC Comics, 1993.

—*The Sandman: The Kindly Ones*. New York: DC Comics, 1996.

—*The Sandman: Preludes and Nocturnes*. New York: DC Comics, 1988.

—*The Sandman: A Season of Mists*. New York: DC Comics, 1992.

—*The Sandman: The Wake*. New York: DC Comics, 1997.

—*The Sandman: World's End*. New York: DC Comics, 1994.

SECONDARY SOURCES:

Amos, Tori. "Introduction." *Death: The High Cost of Living*. New York: DC Comics, 1994, 5-7.

Arendt, Hannah. *Eichmann in Jerusalem: A Report on the Banality of Evil*. London: Russell Square, 1963.

Becker, Ernest. *The Denial of Death*. New York: Free Press Paperbacks, 1973.

Bender, Hy. *The Sandman Companion*. New York: DC Comics, 1999.

Campbell, Joseph. "Editor's Introduction." *The Portable Jung*. Ed. Joseph Campbell. New York: Penguin Books, 1971, vii-xxxii.

—*The Hero with a Thousand Faces*. New York: MJF Books, 1949.

—*The Hero's Journey: Joseph Campbell on his Life and Work*. Ed. Phil Cousineau. San Francisco: Harper & Row, 1990.

—*The Masks of God, Vol. 4: Creative Mythology*. New York: Penguin Books, 1968.

—*The Mythic Dimension*. Ed. Antony Van Couvering. San Francisco: HarperCollins, 1967.

—*Myths to Live By*. New York: Penguin Group, 1972.

—*The Power of Myth* with Bill Moyers. New York: Doubleday, 1988.

Caputi, Jane. "On Psychic Activism: Feminist Mythmaking." *The Feminist Companion to Mythology*. Ed. Caroline Larrington. London: Pandora, 1992, 425-440.

Dundes, Alan. *Essays in Folkloristics*. Meerut: Folklore Institute, 1978.

Eliade, Mircea. *The Sacred and the Profane: The Nature of Religion*. Trans. by Willard Trask. San Diego: Harcourt Brace & Co., 1957.

Gilmore, Mikal. "Introduction." *The Sandman: The Wake*. New York: DC Comics, 1997, 9-12.

Guiley, Rosemary Ellen. "Witchcraft as Goddess Worship." *The Feminist Companion to Mythology*. Ed. Caroline Larrington. London: Pandora, 1992, 411-424.

Hollis, James. *Tracking the Gods: The Place of Myth in Modern Life*. Toronto: Inner City Books, 1995.

Jaffe, Lawrence. *Celebrating Soul: Preparing for the New Religion*. Toronto: Inner City Books, 1999.

Johnson, Robert. *The Fisher King & The Handless Maiden*. San Francisco: HarperCollins Publishers, 1993.

Jung, Carl. *The Archetypes and the Collective Unconscious*. New York: Bollingen Foundation, 1959.

—*Encountering Jung on Mythology*. Ed. Robert Segal.

Princeton: Princeton UP, 1998.

—*Modern Man in Search of a Soul*. San Diego: Hardcourt Brace & Co., 1933.

—*Psychology and Religion*. New Haven: Yale UP, 1938.

Kushner, Ellen. "Neil Gaiman Interview." From National Public Radio's "Sound & Spirit" Program, episode entitled "Dreams," originally aired July 14, 1997.

Larrington, Carolyne. "Introduction." *The Feminist Companion to Mythology*. Ed. Caroline Larrington. London: Pandora,1992, ix-xiii.

Leeming, David Adams. *Mythology: The Voyage of the Hero*. New York: Oxford UP, 1998.

Malinowski, Bronislaw. *Malinowski and the Work of Myth*. Ed. Ivan Stranski. Princeton: Princeton UP, 1992.

McConnell, Frank. "Epic Comics." *Commonweal*. October 20, 1995, v.122, p.21-22.

—"Introduction." *The Sandman: The Kindly Ones*. New York: DC Comics, 1996, 6-11.

—"Preface." *The Sandman: Book of Dreams*. Ed. Neil Gaiman & Ed Kramer. New York: HarperPrism, 1996. 2-6.

Melgrim, Stanley. *Obedience to Authority*. New York: Harper Perennial, 1974.

Mellon, Nancy. *The Art of Storytelling*. Boston: Element Books Unlimited, 1992.

Miller, David. *The New Polytheism: Rebirth of the Gods and Goddesses*. New York: Harper & Row, 1974.

Morrow, Greg, and Goldfarb, David. "The Sandman Annotations." Taken from the web at:
http://rtt.colorado.edu/~jnmiller/Sandman.html

Niebuhr, Reinhold. *The Nature and Destiny of Man*. Volume 1: *Human Nature*. New York: Charles Scribner's Sons, 1941.

—*The Nature and Destiny of Man*. Volume 2: *Human Destiny*. New York: Charles Scribner's Sons, 1943.

Olson, Robert. *An Introduction to Existentialism*. New York: Dover Publications, Inc., 1962.

Ovid. *Metamorphoses*. Trans by A.D. Melville. Oxford: Oxford UP, 1986.

Personal communications with *Sandman* fans.

Real, Terrence. *I Don't Want to Talk About it: Overcoming the Secret Legacy of Male Depression*. New York: Scribner, 1997.

Ricoeur, Paul. *Figuring the Sacred: Religion, Narrative, and Imagination*. Ed. Mark Wallace. Minneapolis: Fortress Press, 1995.

—*The Symbolism of Evil*. New York: Harper & Row, 1967.

Segal, Robert. *Joseph Campbell: An Introduction*. New York: Garland Publishing, Inc, 1987.

Smith, Huston. *Why Religion Matters: the Fate of the Human Spirit in an Age of Disbelief*. San Francisco: HarperCollins Publlishers, 2001.

Straub, Peter. "Afterword: On Mortality and Change." *The Sandman: Brief Lives*. New York: DC Comics, 1994.

Strenski, Ivan. *Malinowski and the Work of Myth*. Ed. Ivan Stranski. Princeton: Princeton UP, 1992.

Stroup, George. *The Promise of Narrative Theology*. Atlanta: John Knox Press, 1981.

Tillich, Paul. *The Courage to Be*. New Haven: Yale University Press, 1952.

Ulanov, Ann. *Religion and the Spiritual in Carl Jung*. New York: Paulist Press, 1999.

Wilson, Terry. "The Big Sleep: Popular 'Sandman' Comic Reaches the End of the Line." *The Chicago Tribune*, November 27, 1995, section C, page 1.

Printed in the United States
27004LVS00003B/34

9 781592 242122